COACH'S GUIDE
TO THE
SLOT I OFFENSE

Gary F. Ray

Parker Publishing Company, Inc. West Nyack, N.Y.

©1974 *by*

Parker Publishing Company, Inc.
West Nyack, N.Y.

Library of Congress Cataloging in Publication Data

Ray, Gary F
  Coach's guide to the slot I offense.

    1. Football--Offense. 2. Football coaching.
I. Title.
GV951.8.R38   796.33'22   74-11291
ISBN 0-13-139410-X

Printed in the United States of America

Dedication

To my wife, Cathy, and my children, John and Jodi, in appreciation for their years of sacrifice, patience, and love, so that I might remain in my chosen profession; and to my parents for their help in my gaining an education, allowing me to follow a coaching career.

What This Book Offers the Coach

High Schools are going increasingly to the I formation, and the contents of this book will cover the Slot I offense from the basic formations through the entire running and passing offenses. I have also included our entire kicking game which I consider a vital part of any good offensive attack.

Written with the high school coach in mind, this book considers such things as small coaching staffs, lack of time, and the player material that is available in the smaller high schools, while still being valuable to the largest programs.

The Slot I offense is explained in detail, including important coaching points that make the offense go. In Chapters 1 and 2, you will find our offensive philosophy, the reasons that we like to use the Slot I formation and the advantages of flip-flopping our entire offensive line and slotback. Also, the four basic offensive formations that we use are diagrammed both to the right and to the left. This part of the book also covers such things as line splits, backfield alignments, hole-numbering system and the huddle.

Chapters 3 and 4 are important ones because they give you the methods of selecting and placing the personnel so that the Slot I offense can be a successful offense for you. In these chapters, you will also find the methods for calling plays and a definition of the terms used in our blocking rules.

In Chapters 5 through 9, the entire Slot I running offense is given. Each chapter takes a backfield position and shows all the offense plays that can be run from that position. All blocking rules and backfield actions are diagrammed from both a left and a right formation. We have diagrammed the right formation against a wide tackle 6-2 defense and the left formation against an Oklahoma 5-4 defense to show the running attack against both an odd and even front defense. Chapter 5 also includes our version of the triple option from the Slot I formation.

Chapters 10 and 11 give our entire sprint out passing series. Chapter 10 covers our basic pass routes and patterns and Chapter 11 includes the backfield action necessary to run our sprint-out passing attack.

Chapter 12 gives you our entire kicking game from punt formation to field goal formation. Also included of course are the kickoff formations, onside kicks and the quick kick. During the past four seasons, we have had only two punts in 96 attempts blocked using our punt formation and those two punts were blocked with sophomores in the game. Included, too, are the coverages that have not allowed a punt or kickoff to be returned for a TD in four years.

Gary F. Ray

Contents

Choosing and Placing Slot I Personnel *(Continued)*

Backfield Personnel:

Play Call:

COACH'S GUIDE
TO THE
SLOT I OFFENSE

1

Advantages of the Slot I Offense

This chapter spells out our offensive philosophy, the advantages of combining the Slot formation with the I backfield and the reasons for flip-flopping our entire offensive formation.

THE OFFENSIVE OBJECTIVES

The major objective of any offense is to move the football down the field enabling us to score. If we cannot move the football by running and/or passing, then the only alternative we have is to give the football to our opponents by means of a kick.

As football coaches, each and every one of us must develop an offensive philosophy. We must ask ourselves: Are we going to move the football on the ground by being a running team or are we going to throw the ball and be a passing team? Although we all attempt to have a balanced attack, we believe any team can be classified as primarily a running or a passing team. Every team does one more than the other.

Although our basic philosophy has changed over the past few years, we would still have to consider ourselves as predominantly a running team. A few years ago, we felt that if we had to pass our offense was definitely in trouble. Now, however, we find ourselves passing more in order to control the defenses that are being played against us. Without a passing threat, we were facing nine-man defensive fronts almost entirely and as you know this definitely makes it tougher on your running attack.

We now feel that an offensive attack must be based upon two things: running and passing the football. They go together and must complement each other in all respects. An offensive team must pass in order to keep the defensive team from putting all its strength on or very near the line of scrimmage. A team must be able to move the football on the ground by means of a consistent running attack to keep the defense from defending against only the passing attack.

WHY THE SLOT I FILLS THE ORDER

With the above in mind, we decided upon the Slot I offensive attack. Our Slot I attack aims to gain yardage with each play and if executed perfectly there is a good chance for a long gainer and a possible touchdown.

We decided on the Slot I offense because passing strength is provided on one side, the slot side, and running strength is provided on the other side, the tight end side. Over the years, we have found that we can run very effectively to the slot side.

Advantages of the Slot Formation

1. *It spreads the defense on the slot side.* Our basic reason for the slot formation was that we wanted the split end wide to force adjustments in the two-deep, nine-man front defenses that we normally faced. We also found that people playing three-deep, eight-man fronts had to make adjustments in their secondaries. The slot back was kept in tight so that we could use him as a blocker and a runner as well as a pass receiver. We seldom split the tight end because we want to maintain blocking leverage to that side.

2. *Varied passing attack.* Although we have limited our passing attack to the play action or sprint-out type of attack, the Slot I formation could easily be adapted to a drop-back type of attack. The slot gives us a three-receiver—tight end, slotback and split end—passing offense. The slot formation provides easy release from the line of scrimmage for our pass receivers.

3. *Strong running attack.* We have found that the slot formation provides us with four types of blocking schemes. Isolation blocking, where we lead block with the fullback on a

linebacker; power blocking is obtained by pulling a guard and leading with the guard, fullback, and sometimes the quarterback; a strong trapping game in which we trap with our guard most of the time but do sometimes pull and trap with a tackle; and a veer or option attack usually to the split end side.

The slotback is always in a good position to block, run, and release for passes. By using the slotback as a ball carrier, we can get good counters, fakes, and reverses both inside and outside.

The slot formation lends itself well to the inside trapping game and has also proved quite successful outside the slotback with power sweeps and options.

By installing our version of the triple option, we feel we have put great pressure on the defensive teams that have tried to play a monster defense on the tight end side.

4. *Much easier to position our personel.* Great specialization can be achieved from your personnel in the slot formation. The split end can be primarily a pass receiver but must also be able to block to the inside. One guard, as you will see later, does almost all pulling and trapping. One back, the tailback, carries the ball 80 percent of the time, etc. Each offensive position, with the exception of the quarterback, must learn only one technique.

Advantages of the I Backfield Formation

1. *Permits a team to feature one great running back.* Many schools are faced with the same problem—that is not being able to find two or three good running backs. The I formation eliminates this problem because no more than one great runner is necessary in this offense. If you are fortunate enough to have two good running backs, it makes the offense twice as tough.

2. *Strong quick-hitting running game.* Not only can the I backfield be highly deceptive but it also reduces the defensive keys. The best ballcarrier can be used to either side of the offensive line. Plays can be run off tackle and outside the end to either side. The I formation enables us to execute the option play better because the quarterback and the tailback are in perfect relationship for an option when the play starts.

Our best blocking back can be used to either side of the offensive line which does not permit teams to stack on one side or the other.

By the mere placement of the backs in the I formation, we can hit any hole without a delay. This gives us increased speed in hitting the hole and does not allow the defensive team more than a split second to adjust.

3. *Reduces defensive keys.* Most defensive teams have a tendency to key the tailback because they know he is the best ball carrier. We have found it is very easy to break the key the defense may be using by sending either the fullback, slotback, or tailback in a direction opposite from the play. Our slotback counters and reverses have been successful enough so that the defensive teams cannot key only on one back.

By combining the advantages of the slot formation with the I backfield, we feel that we have an offensive formation that is second to none. We have found that the Slot I is the ideal formation to use in attacking the ever popular 5-2 monster defenses. The monster must choose a side. He cannot support on the running strength side and then drop off to cover the passing strength side.

Advantages of Flip-Flopping the Formation

1. *Simplicity.* The reason that we flip-flop our entire offensive line and slotback is for simplicity. We have found that better execution of plays is achieved because fewer plays are run. Time spent learning plays is cut in half because there are fewer blocking rules to learn. Two offensive plays, one right and one left, are achieved but only one blocking rule must be learned.

2. *Better utilization of players.* We have also found that we can better utilize the ability of our players by flip-flopping our attack. As an example, the tight-end side guard does more pulling than the slot-side guard. Naturally, the tight end is a completely different technique from the split end, allowing us to use two completely different types of individuals in these positions. We have found it much easier to postion our personnel by flip-flopping our offensive attack.

3. *Permits best blockers against both sides of line.* With every offensive lineman and slotback being flip-flopped, probably the greatest advantage of the Slot I is that it permits the use of

the best offensive blockers against both sides of the defense. If our opponent has a weakness on one side of his defense, we are surely going to find it because we are using our stronger people on both sides.

Many coaches will argue that there is a weakness in flip-flopping the personnel in that it is not quite as easy to develop depth with the flip-flopping of personnel as would be the case in a balanced line that is not flip-flopped. For instance, the next best guard or tackle cannot cover the opposite side position without learning new assignments. We would have to agree with this but as is true in any offense a team cannot have everything.

We feel that the above has made us coach all our players and not just the 14 or 15 better players. With specialization of position involved, we must coach all squad members from sophomores through seniors. The younger players know that they may be called on, which leads to better team unity and better squad morale. Therefore, we definitely feel that flip-flopping has many more advantages than disadvantages.

In summarizing this chapter, the basic offense we arrived at was the Slot I. It seemed to suit our personnel best, it contains most of the things we believed in and that we could coach.

We chose the I because it allowed us to attack from tackle to tackle quickly, enabled the fullback to be used as a lead blocker to both sides, and it is very simple to teach as it involves no complicated backfield actions. It also allows us to feature one great running back at the tailback spot.

We decided to use the slot because we wanted the end split to force adjustments in the eight-and nine-man defensive fronts that we were facing. The slotback was kept in tight so that he could be used as a blocker and runner as well as a pass receiver. We very seldom split the tight end because we want to maintain blocking leverage to his side.

Finally, we used the flip-flop with our linemen and slotback to reduce the time spent teaching blocking assignments and for overall simplicity.

2

Setting Up the Basic Sets and Numbering System for the Slot I Offense

As has been indicated in Chapter 1, our basic offensive formation is the Slot I. Because we flip-flop our entire offensive formation, we have both a right and a left formation. Diagrams 2-1 and 2-2 show the basic slot I formation diagramed to the right and to the left respectively.

The slot side or split end side is always called the strong side of our formation because we have an extra man, the slotback, on that side. The tight end side is called the weak side of our formation. This is also indicated on Diagrams 2-1 and 2-2.

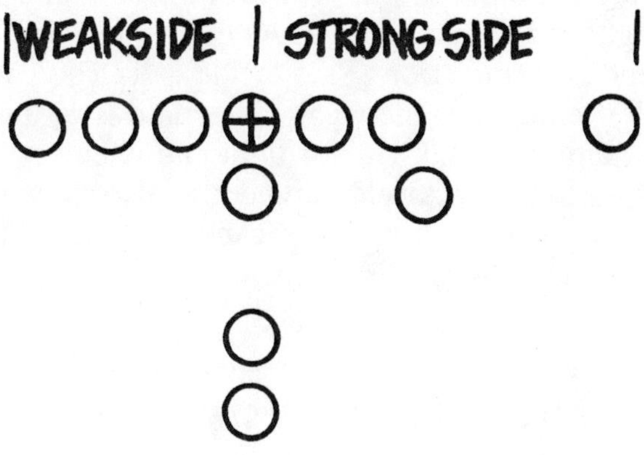

|WEAKSIDE | STRONG SIDE |

Diagram 2-1:
Right Formation

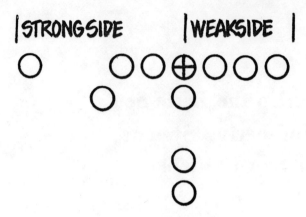

Diagram 2-2: Left Formation

NUMBERING SYSTEM

In our numbering system, we number our personnel rather than the hole. The only exceptions to this are that the areas outside the two offensive ends are also numbered. The area outside the split end is always number 1 and the area outside the tight end is numbered 9. As can be seen in Diagram 2-3 the split end is 2, the strong side tackle is 3. The strong side guard is 4, the center is 5, the weak-side guard is 6, the weak-side tackle is 7, and the weak-side or tight end is 8.

In the backfield numbering, also shown in Diagram 2-3, the slotback is 1, the quarterback is 2, the fullback is 3, and the tailback is 4.

When we use a left formation, the numbering system is also flip-flopped as is shown in Diagram 2-4.

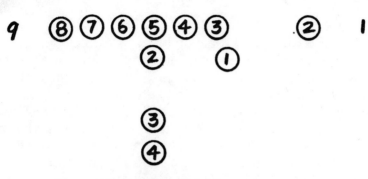

Diagram 2-3: Right Formation

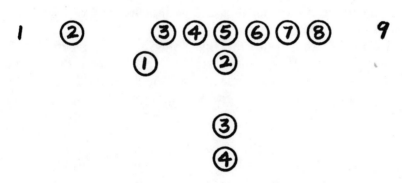

Diagram 2-4: Left Formation

We feel that by using the numbering system shown in Diagrams 2-3 and 2-4 we have simplified our play calling. In Chapter 4, we will go into detail and explain how this numbering system is used to call both a running play and a passing play.

LINE SPLITS

Because we run the triple option, it is extremely important for our offensive linemen to take the same split every time. Our guards, 4 and 6, must take a constant 2-foot split from the feet of the offensive center. The guard splits are very important because our fullback shoots for the guard's outside hip on the option play. We find that very few individuals have a good idea of what two feet or three feet is, therefore, in our pre-season work, we constantly drill merely upon taking the correct splits. Even when the season has started, we drill daily and constantly stress the importance of the correct splits to our linemen because they are so important to the success of the triple option.

On the strong side, our basic splits are 2 feet between the center 5 and the strong side guard 4; a 3 foot split between the 4 guard and the strong side tackle 3; and from 5 to 8 yards between the 3 tackle and the split end 2.

On the weak side, the line splits are 2 feet between the center 5 and the weak-side guard 6; 3 feet between the 6 guard and the weak-side tackle 7; and also 3 feet between the 7 tackle and the weak-side or tight end 8 (Diagram 2-5).

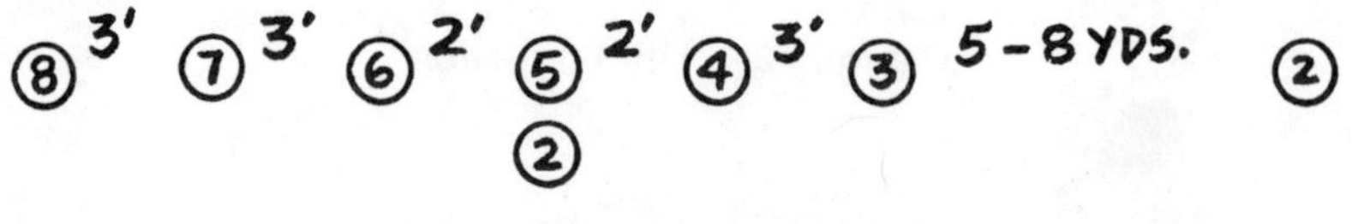

Ⓐ$^{3'}$ Ⓖ$^{3'}$ Ⓕ$^{2'}$ Ⓔ$^{2'}$ Ⓓ$^{3'}$ Ⓒ $^{5-8\,YDS.}$ Ⓑ

Ⓑ

Diagram 2-5: Line Splits

Again, we run a huddle to formation drill every day and check to see that our linemen are taking the proper splits. In early season we spend about five minutes a day and as the season goes on we probably spend from two to three minutes a day drilling on the proper splits and alignments.

BACKFIELD ALIGNMENTS

Because of the triple option, it is also very important that our fullback lines up the same way every time. We use a basic rule of four and ½ yards behind the tip of the ball for the fullback. Adjustments may have to be made from the fullback rule depending upon the fullback's quickness, speed, etc. You may even have one fullback at 4 yards and another at 5 yards depending upon their characteristics. Timing between the fullback and the quarterback is so important that the alignment should be checked daily.

The tailback is a yard behind the fullback. This puts the tailback about 5 to 6 yards deep and in a position to go right or left with ease. Adjustments can be made here to take care of different characteristics of the tailbacks. If you have a slower tailback, cheat him up right behind the fullback. If the tailback has speed to burn, put him deeper and allow him more time to pick the hole or route.

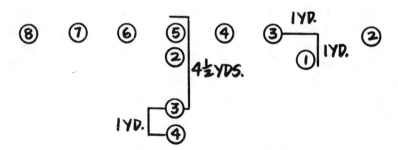

Diagram 2-6: Backfield Alignment

The slotback always aligns a yard outside and a yard behind the 3 tackle. In this position, he can be used as a blocker; he can be used as a ball carrier on a counter or reverse; or he can release downfield on a pass pattern.

STANCE

All interior linemen from the 3 tackle to the 7 tackle are using a 4-point stance. They must have a balanced stance with an even weight distribution and not too much weight forward. The head should be up so that they can see what the defense is doing. Because we flip-flop, they must be able to start with equal ability to their right and to their left. We believe that the 4-point stance, with their feet parallel and not staggered in any way, facilitates their going right and left much more than the 3-point stance.

We allow the 8 end to use either a 3- or a 4-point stance. We feel that it is difficult for the end to release on a pass pattern from a 4-point stance but if this can be done by the 8 end we certainly encourage the 4-point stance. The 8 end is also flip-flopped and the 4-point stance would allow him to go right or left more readily than the 3-point stance.

Now let us consider the stance of our split end. The split end's stance is a funny looking one. His feet are exactly parallel, they are fairly wide and all of his weight is on the feet. The heels are on the ground. He is in a 3-point stance with the hand barely touching the ground. Heels are right on the ground, and the head is up because the primary objective of our split end is to be able to release in, out, or downfield, so we have put him in a stance that will allow him to do this mechanically. If we can get another stance that is better, we will go ahead and use it but this is the best that we have found so far.

As far as the backfield is concerned, the stance of our slot-back is exactly like that of the split end. The slotback must block inside, release outside, and be able to release downfield. Again, the stance described for the split end mechanically allows for these three things.

Our fullback's stance is very important. He must be in a 4-point stance. He must be balanced and he must have an even weight distribution with not too much weight forward. He must be able to start with equal ability to his right and to his left. If his feet are staggered in any way, he will not be able to go in either direction with equal ability. We also want a stance that will allow him to run a straight line. We do not want him to be weaving or getting off path and the 4-point stance allows this.

Our tailback's stance is probably the simplest to teach. We use the upright 2-point stance with the feet parallel. Again, the tailback as well as the fullback must be able to go right or left with equal ability and only a parallel stance will allow this. We have him place the hands on his knees, looking straight ahead. We do not want the hands putting a lot of weight on the feet so we have our tailbacks place the fingers on the inside of the knee and the thumbs on the outside of the knee. We feel that this keeps the tailback from forcing too much weight onto his feet.

As far as the quarterback is concerned, we use the standard quarterback stance. The stance should be comfortable with the feet about shoulder width apart. A parallel or slightly staggered stance, no more than toe to instep, is taught to all our quarter-backs. Most of his weight should be on the balls of his feet. The knees are slightly bent, depending upon the height of the center and the quarterback. Above all else, the quarterback should be in a comfortable, relaxed stance.

As long as we are concerned with the quarterback, let us cover the center-quarterback exchange. The quarterback's right hand should always be on top, regardless whether he is right or left handed. He should place his right hand under the center's crotch with enough upward pressure on the center so the center will feel a target to aim for. The quarterback's thumbs should be placed together and pointing out left. The purpose of the left hand is to stop the center from hiking the ball too far back. It serves as a backboard and stops the ball.

The fingers are slightly curled and both hands should automatically grasp the football when it is snapped by the center. Make sure the quarterback is receiving the ball with the strings up so he will be ready to throw the ball without any unnecessary ball handling.

The centers and quarterbacks should constantly work before and after practice to perfect this exchange. Everything starts with the snap, therefore, it must be an automatic exchange. There is no excuse for a poor center-quarterback exchange.

BASIC FORMATION

As was stated earlier, our basic offensive formation is either a Slot I right (Diagram 2-1) or a Slot I left (Diagram 2-2). However, it is our philosophy that you must run the basic offense from a different formation occasionally. We still run from the Slot I basic formation about 80 percent to 90 percent of the time but to make the defense prepare for more than one offensive formation we do present different looks. We change only one or two people to give the defense a different look. Basically we split the split end wider; we split the tight or 8 end; or we split both the split end 2 and the tight end 8. We change only those two people. Never do we change more than those two.

We use color calls to change from our basic formation to another formation. Again we stress simplicity. A RED call always tells our split end 2 to go wide. By wide we want from 15 to 20 yards between the 2 end and the 3 tackle. It does not matter whether we are in a right or left formation, a red call always splits the 2 end.

A WHITE call always splits the tight end, the 8 end. Again no matter whether he is in a right or left formation on a white call the 8 end will split from 15 to 20 yards.

On a BLUE call both the 2 end and the 8 end split from 15 to

20 yards. We especially like to use this formation against a 5-4-2 Oklahoma defense. It spreads the secondary very thin and allows us to send the slotback up the middle for a long pass play. It also tends to open up the middle area for our running game.

Before we diagram these formations, we will explain how the quarterback calls the formation. In the huddle, the first thing the quarterback calls is the slotback side, either right or left. If he then wants to split people, he makes the appropriate color call, either red, white or blue. He then calls a play such as 41 option which is the triple option. So in the huddle, the quarterback's call might go like this: RIGHT, RED, 41 option. This call tells the linemen that the strong side is right, that the 2 end splits, and that the play, is the 41 option. We will now diagram our formations giving the appropriate call.

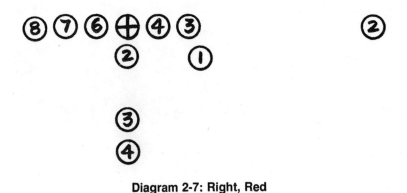

Diagram 2-7: Right, Red

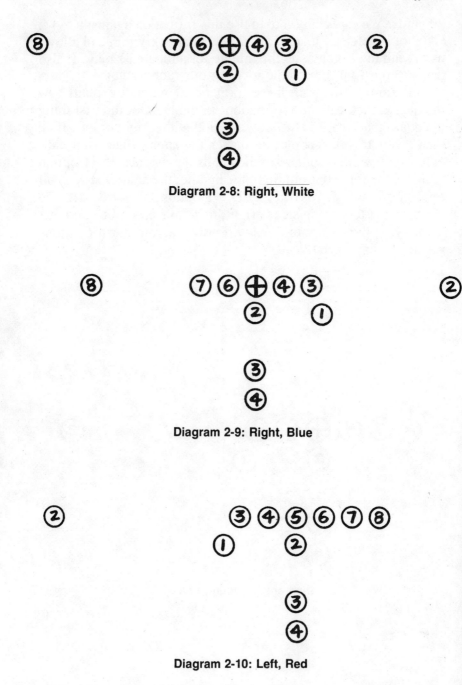

Diagram 2-8: Right, White

Diagram 2-9: Right, Blue

Diagram 2-10: Left, Red

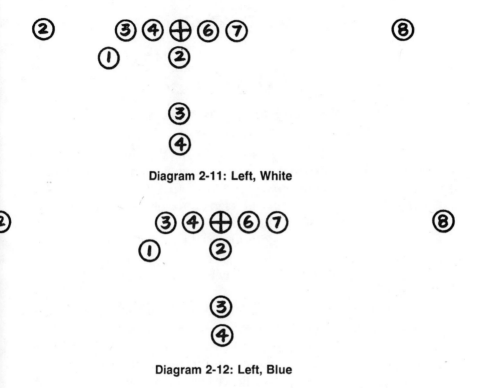

Diagram 2-11: Left, White

Diagram 2-12: Left, Blue

HUDDLE

The last thing that we would like to cover in this chapter is our huddle. We use a closed, rectangular-shaped huddle. The center is responsible for aligning the huddle on the ball and 10 yards away from the ball. On the line of scrimmage side, the center is the middle man, to his right are the 6 guard and the 7 tackle; to his left are the 4 guard and the 3 tackle, giving us five men across the front line. Our 2 end lines up at a right angle to the line of scrimmage next to the 3 tackle, and our 8 end lines up at a right angle to the line of scrimmage next to the 7 tackle. On the back line and facing the five linemen, starting with the 2 end side, we have our slotback, quarterback, fullback, and tailback. (Diagram 2-13)

Diagram 2-13: Basic Huddle

In the huddle, the quarterback calls the play once, then the center leaves. The front four linemen then step together and the quarterback calls the play again. After the second time, the quarterback yells break, everyone claps once and goes to the proper place on the line of scrimmage.

Going from the huddle to a right formation is a very easy task because no one must cross in front of or behind another person. Diagram 2-14 shows how to go from the huddle to a right formation.

In going from the huddle to a left formation, players must cross in front of and behind one another. Remember, the center always leaves early after the play has been called once and before the quarterback repeats the play. We use a rule that the strong side personnel goes first so the 4 guard is the next to go. The 6 guard then crosses behind the 4 guard, then the 3 tackle goes behind the 6 guard; the 7 tackle then goes behind the 3 tackle; the 2 end goes behind the 7 tackle; the 8 end then goes behind the 2 end until all offensive linemen are in place. The slotback goes behind the huddle when a left formation is called. He can leave with the center if it is necessary. The quarterback, fullback, and tailback then step up into their respective places in the offense. It all sounds rather complicated, but with a little drill it becomes a very easy task. Getting from the huddle to the correct formation is practiced along with the alignment drill that we mentioned earlier. Diagram 2-15 shows how to get from the huddle to a left formation. The solid lines always go first, and then the dotted lines cross behind the solid lines. Remember they go alternately—the 4 guard, then the 6 guard, etc.

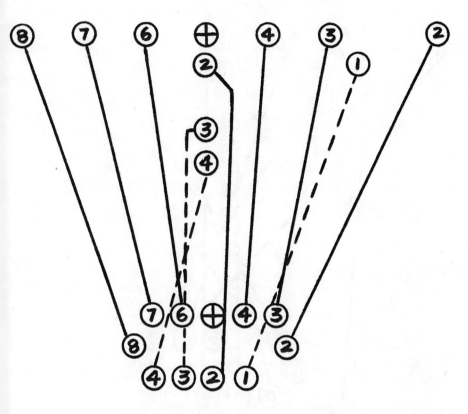

Diagram 2-14: Huddle to Right Formation

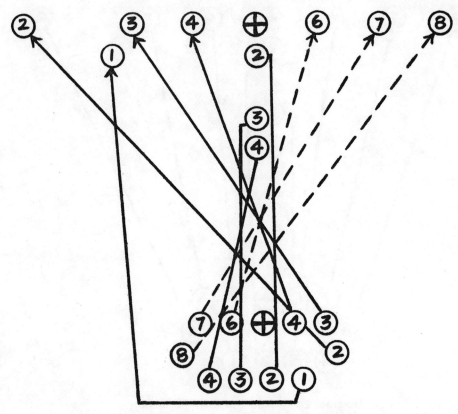

Diagram 2-15: Huddle to Left Formation

3

Choosing and Placing Slot I Personnel

One of the most important, and perhaps the most difficult, aspect of coaching is the proper selection of players for the positions at which they are best suited and where they will perform most effectively. We have often heard that in order to win consistently it is absolutely necessary to have an offense that is suited to the personnel that one has available. In other words, if your personnel does not fit the offense, you should change to another offense that your personnel will better fit.

Our coaching staff was not entirely in agreement with the above idea or philosophy of football. When we were first looking for a sound offensive system, one of the prime considerations was that we wanted an offense that could not only utilize our current personnel but one to which we could adjust almost any personnel, too.

We feel that our Slot-I offense is such an offense. It can be used successfully with many different types of personnel. The past few years, we have been successful with big, slow personnel and we have also been successful with small, quick personnel. We definitely feel that you can take any type of personnel and adjust them to the Slot-I offense.

When examining our personnel for the current season, the very first thing that we do is decide whether they are linemen or backfield personnel. This is usually a rather easy task because the bigger, slower people are probably linemen and the smaller, quicker people are more than likely backs. We do continually recheck to make sure that we have placed them in the proper category, especially with our younger personnel, freshmen and sophomores.

Having completed this initial placement, linemen or backs, we then set about the task of specific positioning of the personnel. It does not matter which category you take first, so we will consider the linemen first. The order in which they are listed is the order of importance, by position, that we use when choosing the positions.

6 Guard

This guard is the key to the success of a good offense and is the most important line position. Quickness and a love of contact are the two prime requirements for this position. The 6 guard will pull and trap or pull and lead on about 95 percent of the running plays. This is why quickness is so important. He must be able to get the job done quickly so as not to mess up the timing in the backfield.

The 6 guard must also love contact because unless he blocks someone every play the offense is not going to work as it is supposed to work. He must pull and trap defensive tackles, he must kick out the defensive ends, and he must lead-block through the hole on the linebackers so he must love contact.

Size is not one of the prime requirements, but because of the people that he must block it surely helps. One of the best 6 guards that we have ever had weighed only 160 pounds but he was very quick and loved contact. He would go out of his way to block people.

Again the characteristics in order of importance are. (1) quickness and mobility; (2) love of contact; (3) size.

7 Tackle

The 7 tackle is the second offensive line position that we select. His most important asset should be quickness and mobility because his main responsibility is pulling and sealing for the 6 guard. Some people call this a cut-off block. He must have the mobility to fill the hole that the pulling guard leaves.

The 7 tackle should be your smaller tackle because getting

off with the count, making contact, and sustaining that contact are more important than brute physical strength. He will also have to be able to block one-on-one.

We have utilized many people between 170 and 180 pounds in this position. The more size that you have, the better one-on-one blocker you will probably have but, again, the prime requisite of the 7 tackle is that he be able to hit quickly and with authority.

5 Center

While some people select the center first because he initiates every offensive play with the snap, we feel that any player with some degree of coordination can become an excellent center. When choosing our center personnel, we look for two things; quickness and coordination.

Of course the center's primary function is the center-quarterback exchange. He must be able to snap the ball quickly and with authority if the offense is going to perform with any degree of consistency. The center should have the quickest reflexes of any offensive linemen so that the ball is snapped before the other linemen jump offside.

Another requirement of the center is that he be able to snap the ball 12 yards deep to our punter. This requires a certain amount of strength but through practice one can acquire the strength necessary to get a good snap.

Another important requirement of the center is that he should be a good one-on-one blocker. He must be able to handle the blocking end or, no matter what kind of a snapper he is, he will not make a good center. He should be able to pick up any blitzing linebacker so here again quickness plays an important part in selecting the center.

We recommend looking for the following characteristics when selecting your centers; (1) quickness; (2) coordination; (3) strength; and (4) size.

4 Guard

In selecting our 4 guard, we feel that strength is of primary importance. The 4 guard does almost entirely one-on-one blocking and of course strength is necessary to provide a good one-on-one block. Along with strength goes size. The 4 guard should have good size but still have some degree of quickness.

On our counters and reverses, we do pull the 4 guard so he must have some degree of mobility and quickness but these are secondary requirements because this is not his primary responsibility.

3 Tackle

The 3 tackle should be the biggest, slowest lineman on the offensive line. The primary requirement of a 3 tackle is size. His blocking is based entirely on size and strength. He will, in many cases, post-block for the slotback to do the driving on a double-team block. He must have size enough so that the defensive tackles cannot drive him back onto the paths of the pulling guard or the quarterback.

This is the place for the slowest linemen on the team because he very rarely goes more than a step or two for his block. He must be able to stop all penetration by the defensive people so again size and strength are of primary importance.

Select your 3 tackles on (1) size; (2) strength; and (3) quickness.

2 End

Since the 2 end will often have to block inside on a linebacker or release downfield on a defensive halfback, speed and aggressiveness are the primary requirements of the 2 end. Both of our ends are chosen on their blocking ability first and their pass-catching ability second. We are primarily a running team, so the ends must always be blockers first.

The 2 end must be able to cut down a pursuing linebacker as well as block a defensive halfback one-on-one. Size is not of primary importance but it will help because the 2 end will often have to block the linebacker. To ask the end constantly to block a linebacker you must be sure that he loves contact and that he will be agressive.

When considering your 2 end candidates, consider speed and quickness first, agressiveness second, and pass catching ability third.

8 End

The 8 end definitely should be selected on his blocking ability first. He must do a lot of one-on-one blocking on plays to the weak side and a lot of downfield blocking on plays to the strong side. He should have some degree of speed for his downfield blocking but his main concern is for one-on-one blocking on the weak side. We use a rather large person here because we feel size and strength are necessary for a good one-on-one block.

The tight end need not be a great pass receiver because almost 90 percent of the time we throw the football to the split end and slotback side of the field. The 8 end, then, is mainly used as a decoy on pass patterns. He is used to keep the defensive secondaries from rotating to the slot side too quickly.

BACKFIELD PERSONNEL

Having covered the offensive line, we will now cover the offensive backfield. As was stated earlier, one of the reasons that we like the Slot I is that it allows us to feature one great running back, the tailback. We will now set about the task of choosing and placing our backfield personnel and again we list them in the order in which we choose them.

Tailback or 4 Back

The tailback must be the best running back that you have available. He will be carrying the football to both sides of the line and will also be carrying the football on about 90 percent of the plays that are run. He must be a strong individual physically because if he is not he will not last the season without injury. He should possess quickness in getting to the hole as well as above average speed in the open field. He must be capable of gaining at least 4 to 5 yards everytime that he carries the football. Size is not one of the prime requirements of the tailback, but as we said earlier, he must be physically strong to be able to take all the contact that he will encounter during a ball game.

Our tailback must be a very durable athlete. If he can throw the football, we can put loads of pressure on the defensive teams by including a pass-run option play with the tailback throwing to the 2 end, or the slotback or by running with the ball himself. We also have our tailback do all the quick-kicking in our Slot I offense.

As you can see, the tailback has to be the best all-around athlete on your football team. His responsibilities require him to be one of the team leaders as well as the team's leading ball carrier.

Fullback or 3 Back

When selecting our fullback candidates, we basically look for only two traits. They are (1) physical strength, and (2) desire to hit. A good fullback must have these two traits because of his responsibilities in the Slot I offense. Many times he will be responsible for kicking the defensive end out or lead-blocking through a hole on the linebacker. Size is not too important if he has the strength to block these defensive people. Of course the more size he does have the better all-around football player he will be.

Another quality that the fullback must have is the ability to carry the football on the short trapping game. He must be a threat to the defense on the inside if the triple option, the sweep, etc. are going to work on the outside with the tailback carrying the football.

Again, when selecting the fullback look for the two qualities of physical strength and a desire to hit. If your fullback has these two things, you definitely can make him a fine blocker as well as a fine ball carrier for the inside running game.

Quarterback or 2 Back

Leadership is the key to a good quarterback candidate. He must possess a strong commanding voice that will make him a forceful and respected team leader. He must be the team leader both on and off the football field. Our coaching staff looks for the individual who is capable of making things happen on and off the field. The quarterback is the coach of the offensive team on the field and, therefore, he must be one who can make the team move and score. He must always be a confident leader and in order to possess this confidence he must have enough intelligence to understand the entire offensive system. It is the quarterback's responsibility to lead the offense downfield and in for the score. He must have a certain degree of poise and common football sense to be able to select the correct play at the right moment.

Courage is another important trait that a quarterback must have. We believe that all football players have a certain amount of courage but the quarterback, as the leader, must have the courage to stand up for his teammates, the courage to stand behind the play that he has called regardless of the outcome, and the courage to follow the game plan to the end.

Up to this point, we have been considering mental qualities of a good quarterback. Now let's consider the qualities of a good quarterback from a physical standpoint.

Physically, the quarterback must be a good ball handler with quick hands and feet. The quarterback must possess a certain amount of speed to enable him to execute all the plays consistently. He must be physically able to run with the football as well as being able to throw it accurately. Size is not as important as one might think. We have had quarterbacks 5'7" who have been outstanding players. We do feel, however, that if you have two people of equal ability, the taller of the two will probably be the better quarterback because he is in a better position to see defensive personnel over your own offensive line.

Slotback or 1 Back

The actual positioning of the slotback makes him somewhat of a unique person. He must be a blocker, runner, and a pass receiver. In our offense, we always consider first the thing that he will do most often. Therefore, we consider the slotback as a blocker first, a runner next, and finally as a pass receiver. The slotback is actually a combination of the fullback and the 2 end. He will do an enormous amount of double-team blocking with the 3 tackle, and, therefore, must have the physical strength to complete the double-team block successfully. He must have a certain amount of quickness in order to complete the double-team block before the defensive man gets by the 3 tackle. He must possess a love of contact because this is what he will be doing most of the time, contacting the defensive tackles.

As a runner, he must have speed and quickness. He will be carrying the ball on counters and reverses and, therefore, will not need the overpowering strength of say a fullback. When the slotback carries the football, we are usually trying to fool the defense.

Finally, as a pass receiver, the slotback should possess speed and quickness along with a good set of hands. He must be able to complete the pass route quickly and then be able to catch the football if it is thrown to him.

In summarizing this chapter, remember that the keys to a successful Slot I offense are the 6 guard, the tailback, and the quarterback in that order. These three people should always be considered first.

Also, remember that any personnel can be adapted to this offense if careful consideration is given when selecting them.

4

Determining Play Calling and Blocking Rules for the Slot I

The method that will be used for communication purposes is one of the most important phases of any football offense. A communication system must be simple enough for all persons involved, coaches, quarterbacks, and players to understand but yet complicated enough to convey the information necessary to run a successful offense. A sound communication system must include the following things: a method of calling a running play; a method of calling a passing play; and a set of blocking rules; so that the offensive players understand immediately what is wanted. Let us now consider each of these things individually.

CALLING THE RUNNING PLAY

In calling a running play, our quarterbacks must give the offensive personnel the following information: (1) direction; (2) formation; (3) play desired; and (4) the snap count. As far as direction is concerned, the quarterback has only two choices—either right or left. These formations were diagrammed in Chapter 2 (Diagrams 2-1 through 2-4), but briefly as a review, the right formation has the split end, 2 end, and the slotback, 1 back, on the right side of the offensive formation and in the left formation the split end and the slotback are on the left side of the formation. Having decided upon the direction, the first thing the quarterback relays to the offensive team is the direction desired—either right or left.

The next information that must be given to our offensive personnel is the formation desired by the quarterback. Here the quarterback actually has four choices: (1) normal; (2) red; (3) white; and (4) blue. If a normal formation is desired as shown in (Diagrams 2-1 and 2-4), the quarterback merely skips a formation call. His call would then include a direction, play, and snap count. As an example, a sample call by the quarterback might be Right, 41, on 2. This call would tell our offensive personnel that the quarterback wants a right, normal formation and he wants to run play 41 on 2. If a formation other than a normal formation is wanted, then the quarterback must relay the desired formation in his call. As an example, the quarterback might make the following call in the huddle: Right, Red, 41 on 1. That particular call would tell the offensive team that the desired direction is right; it would tell the 2 end or split end to split wide; that the desired play is a 41 and that the snap count is 1. A Left, White, 41, on 2 would tell our offensive players that the desired direction is left; that the 8 end or tight end splits wide; that the desired play is a 41; and that the snap count is 2. The only other formation call that the quarterback might use would be a Blue call which would split both the 2 end and the 8 end. An example of this call might be Left, Blue, 41 on 2.

Notice again the simplicity of our formation calls. The only people concerned with the formation call are the 2 end and the 8 end. Only these two people move to give us a different formation.

The third bit of information that is given by the quarterback is the play. Our running plays consist of a two-digit number such as a 41. The first digit tells which back is going to carry the football, and the second digit tells the area or hole that he is going to run through. The 41 call would tell our tailback (4 back) that he will carry the ball and that he should go outside the 2 end or to the 1 area. Another sample play call might be a 33. This call tells our fullback (3 back) that he will carry the ball over the 3 tackle or the 3 hole. We have found this to be a very simple, yet successful, system of calling plays because it tells which back will carry the football and also what area he should run to.

The fourth and final information that the quarterback should give to our offensive personnel is the snap count. He must tell the offensive players when to move or when to start the play. He may use any snap count from set on up to 3. However, about 98 percent of our offensive plays are run on 1 or 2. Our snap count or cadence will be explained in more detail later in this chapter.

Now, before moving to the calling of a passing play, let's review the entire information given by the quarterback in the huddle to the offensive players. As an example, Right, Red, 41 on 2, tells the offensive personnel that the desired direction is right, that the desired formation is a Red formation (2 end splits wide); that the desired play is a 41 (the tailback around the right end) and that the snap count will be on two.

CALLING THE PASSING PLAYS

When calling a passing play, our quarterbacks still give our offensive personnel the same four things; (1) direction; (2) formation; (3) play; and (4) snap count. The first, second, and fourth items remain the same as in calling a running play. However, the third item, the play, is changed. When calling a running play, we used a two-digit number, so in calling a passing play we use a three-digit number, such as 133. As you will see in Chapter 10, we number our pass patterns using three digits as 100, 200, 300, 400, etc. The first digit in the play call, 133, tells our receivers to run a 100 pattern and the next two digits tell our backfield personnel what running play we would like them to fake, in this case a 33.

A complete passing play call given in the huddle by the quarterback would go like this: Right, Blue 133, on 1. A call such as this would tell the offensive players that the desired direction is right, the formation desired in blue (both ends split); that the desired pattern is a 100 pattern for the receivers; the desired backfield action is a 33; and that the snap count will be on 1.

For simplicity then, the only difference between a running play and a passing play would be using a two-digit number instead of a three-digit number. Any time our offensive linemen hear a three-digit number, they know that they cannot release downfield until the ball is thrown.

CADENCE

Our cadence or snap count is non-rhythmic in nature. We make use of only two terms in our cadence—SET and GO. In order to use this type of cadence, we must constantly drill so that our people will always react in the same way. Upon leaving the huddle, all offensive personnel must go to their proper positions and bend at the waist, placing their hands on their knees. The only exceptions to this are the center, who goes over the ball so that he can snap the ball immediately, and the quarterback, who goes under the center ready to receive the snap. By aligning in this manner, we can use the word SET for a quick snap count. When using SET as a quick snap count, our offensive players fire out from the hands on knees position.

If we are not using SET as a quick snap count, on SET our personnel assume the correct stance for their position. Our quarterback must then repeat the word GO the correct number of times that he called in the huddle. As an example, if the quarterback had called the play on 1, he would then make the following voice calls at the line of scrimmage—SET, GO in a non-rhythmic progression. If the call of the play was on 3, the quarterback's voice calls at the line of scrimmage would be——SET, GO, GO, GO in a non-rhythmic pattern.

Again, as we mentioned earlier, about 98 percent of our plays are run on 1 or 2. The other 2 percent on SET or 3. We definitely like to go on 1 the majority of the time because it helps eliminate offsides, motion, etc.

AUTOMATIC SYSTEM

We do not believe in the automatic system and we do not allow our quarterbacks to call an automatic away from a particular play at the line of scrimmage. We do a thorough job of selling the offense to our players and, therefore, we feel that the use of automatics would defeat our purpose. We sell our players on the idea that any of our offensive plays can gain yardage against any defense if we execute and block the play properly. To allow the quarterback to call an automatic at the line of scrimmage would be contradicting the selling job we have done. It would be telling our people that the play called was no good and, with time, they would lose confidence in the offense and in the quarterback. We are probably the simplest people in the world but we have been successful with our approach and, therefore, we do not want to complicate the offense by using automatics at the line of scrimmage.

BLOCKING RULES

Blocking rules are the most important part of any offensive system. The purpose of any blocking rule is to help the offensive personnel to determine their blocking assignment, for the particular play called. For many years, the most common method of determining the correct assignment was by using the so-called numbering system. In this system, the defensive team was numbered either from the center out or from the defensive end in. If you were supposed to block Number 2, you counted, found player number 2 and tried to block him no matter where he went. Problems arise in trying to count and block stunting defenses, so we like to use what we call a rule blocking system. In this type of a blocking system, we use words to help indicate the proper blocking assignment. As an example, the blocking assignment for our 4 guard may read—Gap, On, Over. This rule would tell the guard to block anyone in the gap first; if no one is in the gap, then block the man on you; or finally, if no man is on you, then block the man over you. The offensive player does not have to survey the entire defensive front and count people to find his blocking assignment. All that is necessary in our rule blocking system is to look at the area immediately next to, or in front of, your offensive position. By surveying this small area and by applying your blocking rule, the person that you are supposed to block can be found very quickly and easily.

The important part of the rule blocking system is to understand what the terms used in the rule mean. We will, at this time, list and define the terms used in our Slot I offensive system of rule blocking. Many of these terms are commonly used and probably need no definitions but to be on the safe side, we will define all those terms that we employ in our Slot I offense.

Gap

Block the defensive lineman in the gap between you and the next lineman toward the offensive center.

On

Block any defensive lineman playing head up on you.

Over

Block any linebacker playing over your position.

Inside

Block the first person on or over the offensive person next to you toward the offensive center. This person might be either a lineman or a linebacker.

Outside

Block the first defensive person outside or away from the center. This person can be either a lineman or a linebacker.

Weak Side

Block toward the tight end or the 8 end side. This is a term usually used in connection with the center's rule.

Strong Side

Block toward the split end or 2 end side. This is normally a term used in connection with the center's blocking assignment.

Lineman

Any defensive person within a yard of the line of scrimmage.

Linebacker

Any defensive person more than one yard and less than five yards from the line of scrimmage.

Halfbacks

Any defensive person more than five yards from the line of scrimmage. These people usually are head up on the offensive ends and from six to ten yards deep.

Safety

Any defensive person over the middle of the defense and more than five yards deep. The safety will normally be about ten yards deep and directly over the offensive center.

Play Side

That side of the offensive line that the play is being run to.

Back Side

The side of the offensive line away from the side that the play is being run to.

Downfield

Release inside the defensive man on or over you and block the first person on the other team that you can get to in the secondary. This term is usually used in connection with the end away from the play.

Pull and Trap

Vacate your position by moving down the line of scrimmage and block (trap) the first defensive man that shows. This is usually the 6 guard's rule and it will include the man you should trap, such as, the first man past 3 (3 tackle).

Pull and Seal

Vacate your position and block the defensive man in the area of the pull and trap man. Usually the 7 tackle's rule where he is sealing or filling the hole left by the pulling 6 guard.

Pull and Lead

Vacate your position by moving down the line of scrimmage and lead or turn up into the hole. Block first off-colored jersey through the hole.

Before leaving blocking rules, we would again like to emphasize the importance of a simple, easily understood blocking rule. The blocking rule should clearly indicate whom the offensive man should block and it in no way should be so complicated that it merely confuses the offensive man. If a blocking rule in any way interferes with the blocking of the offensive personnel, it should be eliminated and replaced with a rule that is more easily understood.

5

Coaching Slot I Tailback Plays

As indicated in Chapter 3, the tailback must be the best running back that you have available because he is the main ball carrier in our Slot I offensive attack. He will, in all probability, be carrying the football about 90 percent of the time and to both sides of the offensive formation. He must be a strong individual physically in order to make it through the football season without injury. He should have quickness in getting to the hole as well as above average speed in the open field. He need not be the overpowering runner who is capable of running over people but he must be capable of gaining at least four or five yards every time that he is called upon to carry the football. As was mentioned earlier, size is not one of the primary requirements of the tailback but he must be capable of enduring the physical contact that he will encounter during the course of the football game.

With the above qualifications of the tailback in mind, we will present our tailback offensive plays for the Slot I offense. We will present each play from both a right and left formation. We will also present each play against two different defenses: first, diagrammed against a wide tackle 6-2 defense from a right formation, and; second, diagrammed against the Oklahoma 5-4 defense from a left formation. By presenting each running play in this manner, we hope to show you two things: (1) the basic play diagrammed against both an odd and even front defense, and (2) how we flip-flop or mirror our offensive running attack—thus getting two running plays but teaching only one set of blocking rules.

We will follow each set of diagrams with the line blocking rules and the backfield assignments. After the backfield assignments, which for the most part are self-explanatory, we will mention a few coaching points concerning the play. Occasionally, we will include a drill that we use to help make a particular play a better play.

Play Call: Right or Left 41 (Diagrams 5-1 and 5-2)

Blocking Rules for Play 41

>2 End—first man to the inside   *1ST MAN INSIDE*
>3 Tackle—gap, over, outside *G°°°*
>4 Guard—gap, over, outside *G°°°*
>5 Center—over, back side   *ON-OVER - W.S.*
>6 Guard—pull and lead (look to the inside)
>7 Tackle—pull and seal for 6 guard *SEAL FOR G...*
>8 End—safety or opposite halfback
>Slotback—protect gap, block first man in slot
>Fullback—first man past 2 end, if he refuses to come across the line, try to hook him in and the tailback will go wide.
>Tailback—ball carrier, do not cut too soon, make your cut off the fullback's block.
>Quarterback—reverse pivot and pitch the ball to the tailback, lead the play through the hole, run a straight line once through the hole, blocking only those who challenge you.

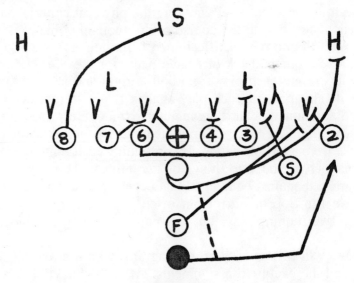

Diagram 5-1

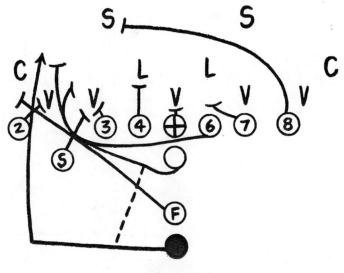

Diagram 5-2

Coaching Points: This play is our bread and butter play in the Slot I offense. We must run this play extremely well in order to make the rest of the offense work effectively. The key to this play is the fullback's block on the person responsible for containment on our opponent's defense. The tailback must read this block before he makes his cut upfield. Timing is of primary importance to this play and we develop timing by running this play against air dummies in early pre-season practice and by live practice in controlled scrimmage situations.

Always have your 6 guard look and block to the inside once he turns the corner so that he can block any pursuing linebackers or linemen. Be sure the 7 tackle is pulling and sealing for the 6 guard—this is a very important assignment and the technique should be checked regularly.

Also, we feel it is often necessary to give the defense a different look offensively, so we like to run this play with the 8 end split (a white formation). We can also split the 2 end (a red formation) but for the most part we keep him in for the blocking power. A red or blue formation can be used occasionally depending upon where the defensive personnel align.

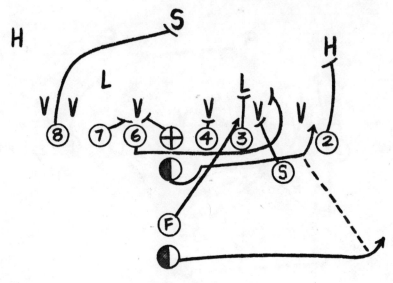

Diagram 5-3

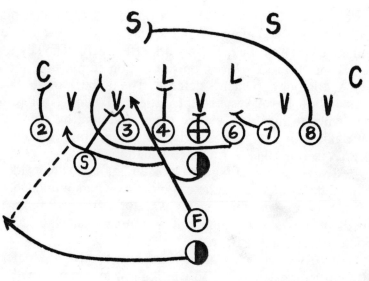

Diagram 5-4

Play Call: Right or Left 41 Belly (Diagrams 5-3 and 5-4)

Blocking Rules for 41 Belly

2 End—release across end, block corner or your halfback *SS*
3 Tackle—gap, over, outside *Gᵒᵒᵒ*
4 Guard—gap, over, outside *Gᵒᵒᵛ*
5 Center—over, back side *ᴼᴺ - ᴼᵛᴱᴿ - ᵂ·ˢ·*
6 Guard—pull and lead (look to the inside)
7 Tackle—pull and seal for 6 guard
8 End—safety or opposite halfback
Slotback—gap, man in slot, linebacker inside
Fullback—fake a 33, block linebacker if possible but make a good fake first
Tailback—ball carrier, run a 41 route, sprint toward sideline, if quarterback turns upfield, keep relationship with him for possible pitch
Quarterback—reverse pivot, get depth, quick fake to the fullback on a 33, run right at the contain man and option him

Coaching Points: Notice that the blocking rules for the linemen, with the 2 end an exception, are exactly the same as the 41 so that no new rules must be taught to the linemen for this play. The fullback must make a good fake to freeze the linebackers and make the option work. We do like to spread the defense for this play so we run it either from a red or a blue formation quite often. In either formation, we instruct the 2 end to streak downfield, trying to take the halfback with him. If the halfback comes up, we do have a 41 pass, that will be given later, to throw to the 2 end going deep.

The next play is our answer to the triple option run from the Slot I formation. We use this play only if the quarterback is capable of reading both the defensive end and the defensive tackle correctly. It takes an enormous amount of practice for the quarterback to execute the triple option correctly. If the quarterback cannot read and execute the triple option, then we use only the 41 belly for our option play. Also, if the defense is making his tackle-end read difficult we will instruct our quarterbacks to use only the 41 belly option.

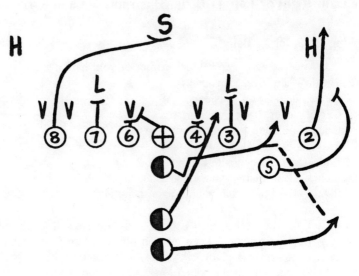

Diagram 5-5

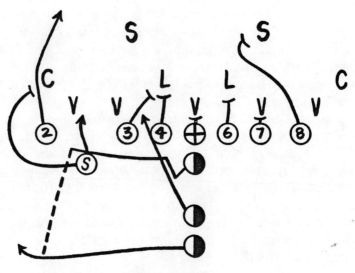

Diagram 5-6

Play Call: Right or Left 41 Option (Diagrams 5-5 and 5-6)

Blocking Rules for 41 Option

2 End—run 100 pass pattern trying to take the defensive halfback with you or block the defensive halfback if he won't follow you

3 Tackle—gap, linebacker *GAP - OVER - LB INSIDE*

4 Guard—gap, over, linebacker *G000*

5 Center—over, back side *ON - OVER - W.S.*

6 Guard—gap, over, linebacker *G000*

7 Tackle—gap, over, linebacker *G000*

8 End—safety or opposite halfback

Slotback—release across the face of the defensive end and block man responsible for outside one third of field

Fullback—run a 33 at the inside hip of the 3 tackle, possible ball carrier so put a soft squeeze on the ball, block the linebacker if you do not get the ball

Tailback—run a 41 route, and maintain pitch relationship with the quarterback as in a 41 belly, always be ready for a pitch from the quarterback

Quarterback—step at a 45 degree angle to the fullback, placing the ball in the fullback's stomach. Read the handoff key (first man outside 3 tackle), if he closes, keep the ball and option the defensive end. If the handoff key goes outside or stays at home, give the ball to the fullback.

Coaching Points: The play of the quarterback makes or breaks this play. The quarterback steps at a 45 degree angle toward the fullback, looking at the first man outside of the 3 tackle and depending upon the defensive man's reaction, he will exercise his first option—if the defensive man plays normal and stays at home, the quarterback will give the ball to the fullback and continue down the line faking his second and third options. If the defensive man converges on the fullback, the quarterback will keep the ball and exercise his second option—determined by the action of the defensive end. If the end elects to cover the quarterback, he should exercise the third option and pitch to the tailback. If the defensive end decides to cover the tailback, the quarterback should keep the ball himself and turn upfield. We also instruct our quarterback not to pitch the ball once he turns upfield on the second option except when he is absolutely sure the tailback will receive a good pitch and gain more yardage than the quarterback currently has gained. We would much sooner take a five yard gain than make a poor pitch and lose yardage.

As for line play, we instruct our 3 tackle always to be sure and leave two option people—the defensive end and the next person inside the defensive end for the quarterback to option. The line splits between the 5 center, 4 guard and 3 tackle are very important to this play and must constantly be checked by the offensive line coach. The splits from the center out must be 2 feet, 3 feet, to give the fullback the proper angle to the quarterback.

We like to use a spread formation for this play to help isolate the defensive players. A red or blue formation would help determine who is responsible for containing the pitch man because the spread formation forces the defense to adjust to the wide people.

Because this is a relatively new idea from the Slot I formation, we would like to give you four drills that we use to develop this particular play—the 41 option or the triple option.

Drill 1: Pressure Drill: Center and quarterbacks are the only ones involved. We use this drill approximately five minutes in pre-season and two to three minutes once the season starts. This is a very simple, but very important, drill. The quarterback cannot worry about the center-quarterback exchange because he must concentrate on the reading of the defense. The quarterback does not have time to look the ball into his hands; he must know ahead of time that the ball will be there correctly. This sureness is developed through practice. To execute the drill, we just line our centers and quarterbacks across the field and have the centers snap the ball to the quarterback as many times as is possible in the time allowed. (Formation for this drill is pictured in Diagram 5-7.)

Drill 2: Pressure—Read Drill: We now add the fullbacks to the pressure drill and make use of a coach or manager to give the

Diagram 5-7: Pressure Drill Formation

quarterback someone to read. A point five feet from the center is marked to give the fullback the proper angle with the quarterback. Make sure the fullback is going over the spot marked every time. Again the quarterback must know where the fullback will be, he will not have time to look for the fullback. We use this drill approximately five minutes in pre-season and two to three minutes once the season starts. The coach or manager should look right into the quarterback's eyes to make sure that the quarterback is reading him and also to see that the quarterback is not looking for or at the fullback. The formation for this drill is given in Diagram 5-8.

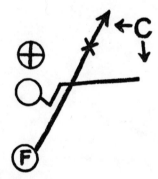

Diagram 5-8: Pressure-Read Drill

Drill 3: Pitch Drill: This drill involves the quarterback and the tailback. The pitch is the next step for the quarterback. He must be able to pitch the ball with either hand and hit the tailback between the waist and the shoulders. Likewise, the tailback needs to practice catching the pitch regardless of where it is pitched. We make the quarterback pitch 25 times with each hand daily in the pre-season and at least 15 times, and preferably 25 times, during the season. As coaches we must constantly check for the proper relationship between the quarterback and the tailback. Diagram 5-9 shows the formation for the pitch drill.

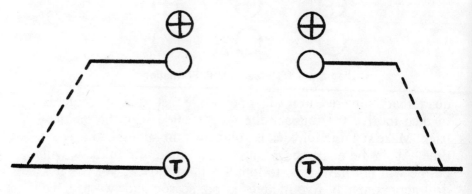

Diagram 5-9: Pitch Drill

Drill 4: Option Drill: We now put the entire option together, using three live defensive people to read and a hand air dummy for the fullback to block if he does not get the ball. The coach

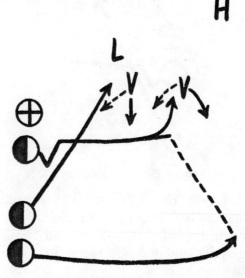

Diagram 5-10: Option Drill

should check all aspects of the triple option to see that they are being performed correctly. We use this drill 25 times to each side daily in pre-season and 15 times to each side during the season, Diagram 5-10 shows the Option Drill alignments.

As can readily be seen, it takes some practice time to perfect the triple option but we feel that the results we have had are worth the practice time spent. If we are not getting results from the triple option, then we quit running the play and quit spending the practice time to perfect it.

Play Call: Right or Left 42 (Diagrams 5-11 and 5-12)

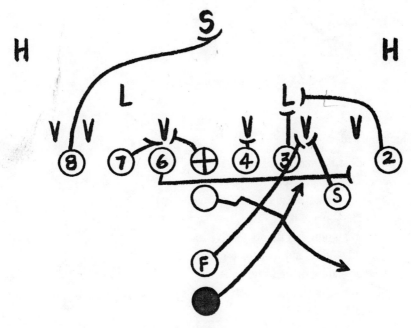

Diagram 5-11

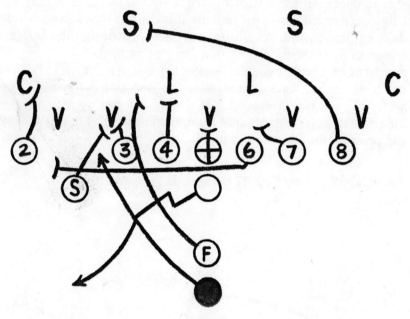

Diagram 5-12

Blocking Rules for 42

2 End—first man to inside   1ST LB OVER, OUTSIDE, INSIDE

3 Tackle—gap, over, outside GOOD

4 Guard—gap, over, outside GOOD

5 Center—over, back side   ON - OVER - W.S.

6 Guard—pull and trap defensive end

7 Tackle—pull and seal for 6 guard

8 End—safety or opposite halfback

Slotback—protect gap, block man in slot, linebacker GOOD

Fullback—fake a 33

Tailback—ball carrier, run at outside hip of 3 tackle

Quarterback—open, fake to the fullback and hand to tailback, set up as if
    to pass

L-O-O

Coaching Points: This play gives us a quick trap off the tackle with usually a double-team block in the tackle area. We added this play so that people who are keying the quarterback might key him incorrectly. This play and the 41 option are the only plays that the quarterback opens at 45 degrees rather than a reverse pivot. Against a 5-4 defense we like to use a red formation if the corner linebacker will go out with the 2 end. A white or blue formation is sometimes advantageous to spread the defense on the back side.

Play Call: Right or Left 45 (Diagrams 5-13 and 5-14)

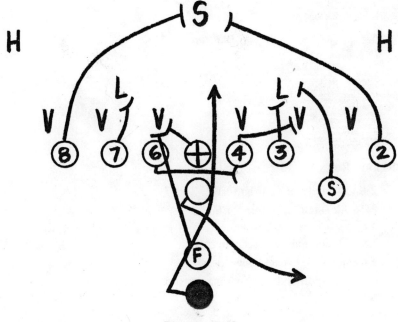

Diagram 5-13

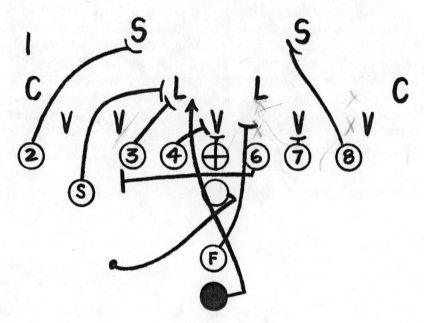

Diagram 5-14

Blocking Rules for 45

    SS, HB

    2 End—safety or your halfback

    3 Tackle—release inside for linebacker   OVER—LB INSIDE

    4 Guard—if man over—block first man to outside, no man over—drive
       ON   1ST MAN OUTSIDE   ON - 1ST MAN
        block man on 5 center

    5 Center—over, back side   OV- OVER- W,S

    6 Guard—pull and trap first man past 5 center

7 Tackle—linebacker, outside *GOOD*

8 End—safety or your halfback *w-is A-O*

Slotback—man over or slightly outside, linebacker inside *INSIDE* *OVER, INSIDE LB.*

Fullback—fake at 6 hole and fill for 6 guard

Tailback—ball carrier, take a jab step to the weak side and run at 5 hole

Quarterback—step at 45 degrees and fake to the fullback and hand back
to the tailback, set up as if to pass

Coaching Points: The faking in the backfield is very important in this play. The quarterback should step at 45 degrees toward the weak side and fake to the fullback; then pivot toward the strong side giving the ball to the tailback. The quarterback should continue out and set up as if to pass. This action by the quarterback tends to stop most of the pursuit by the left defensive people with the offense in a right formation and vice versa, because of the bootleg possibilities. We do not have a special bootleg pass—if we see the end and tackle pursuing too quickly down the line of scrimmage, we tell our quarterback to keep the ball and bootleg to the weak side. The fullback must constantly be reminded of his responsibilities on the play. First, a good fake, and then a block to seal the hole that the 6 guard vacated. This is a very quick-hitting trap play and allows our tailback to gain good yardage before the secondary of our opponents can react. We also like to run this against a defense that will spread with our wide formations: Red, White, or Blue.

The next tailback play in our offense would appear to many as a duplicate of the 45 with a different number. Over the years, we have found that many teams have been keying very heavily on our 6 guard. Therefore, we had to develop a key-breaking play which is why we have a 46 play. We block gap, over, with the 6 guard and pull and trap with the 7 tackle. The play is actually run slightly inside the 6 guard but because we have a 45 we called this play a 46.

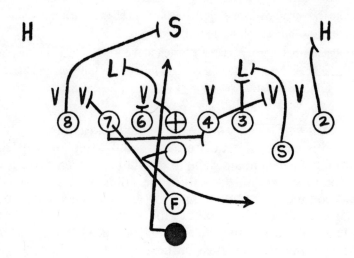

Diagram 5-15

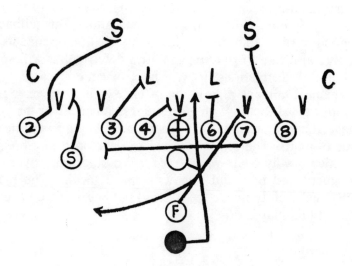

Diagram 5-16

N o

Play Call: Right or Left 46 (Diagrams 5-15 and 5-16)

Blocking Rules for 46

2 End—fake block at first man inside, then go downfield for your half-back

3 Tackle—linebacker inside

4 Guard—drive block man on 5 center, no man on 5, pull and block first man to outside

5 Center—post block man on, no man on—block first man to the weak side

6 Guard—gap, post man on, fill area

7 Tackle—pull and trap first man past 5 center

8 End—safety or your halfback

Slotback—block linebacker inside or man in slot area

Fullback—fill for 7 tackle just past the outside hip of 6 guard, make a good fake with the quarterback

Tailback—jab step weak, then cut as close to double-team block as is possible

Quarterback—step to weak side and give a hand fake to the fullback, then hand to tailback, continue to strong side as if to bootleg

Coaching Points: The timing of this play is extremely important and must be practiced often. The tailback must be shown where the double-team block will be against every defense that you will play against so he will know where his cut should be. Against a 5-man defensive front the double team will be on the 5 center so his cut will be at the outside hip of the 6 guard. Against the 6-man defensive fronts the double-team block will be over the 6 guard, therefore, he must cut at the inside hip of the 6 guard. Also, we teach our centers to do a combination block to use on the wide-tackle 6-2 defense as is shown in Diagram 5-15. He should drive a shoulder into the defensive man over the 6 guard to help set up the guard's block, and then slide on by and pick up the weak-side linebacker. The quarterback's bootleg action tends to freeze the defensive ends and secondary people, allowing a good gain before they can react to the football.

Probably the most reliable play in our entire offensive running game to the weak side has been our 47 play. This is a power play in which the tailback follows the fullback through the 7 hole. It is a very quick hitting play that can break for the long gainer.

Play Call: Right or Left 47 (Diagrams 5-17 and 5-18)

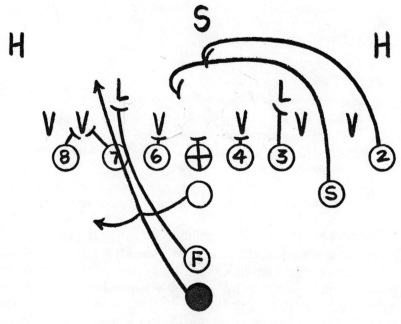

Diagram 5-17

Blocking Rules for 47

  2 End—release inside and fan at hole
  3 Tackle—gap, over, linebacker *Covo*
  4 Guard—gap, over, linebacker *Goo*
  5 Center—strong side gap, over, fill area *on -over - S.S.*

6 Guard—man over, outside G-oo ꙍ

7 Tackle—over, outside   ON - 'oUTSIDE OR X - BLock (You block 2ND)

8 End—gap, man over, first man inside GAP- ON - INSIDE OR X - BLock
  (You BLock 1ST)

Slotback—release inside and fan at hole

Fullback—lead block at the 7 hole looking for the linebacker

Tailback—follow the fullback and cut off his block

Quarterback—step to weak side and hand to the tailback, then set up as if
  to pass

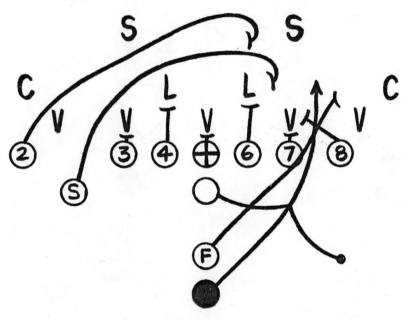

Diagram 5-18

Coaching Points: We have mentioned a new technique on the part of the 2 end and the slotback. By fan at the hole, we want the two blockers to turn to the inside and try to cut off any defensive personnel who might be pursuing from the strong side. This is a very easy technique to teach and it was illustrated in

both Diagrams 5-17 and 5-18. Another thing that we do against
certain defenses that our opponents are using against us is to
cross block with the 7 tackle and the 8 end. When we want to
cross block, our quarterback merely calls 47X. When executing
the cross block, the 8 end always blocks down first and then the 7
tackle blocks to the outside (See Diagram 5-19).

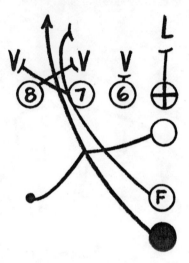

Diagram 5-19

When we can utilize the crossblock technique, we merely
call the play a 47X. No assignments are changed except for the 7
tackle and the 8 end. Also, a good blocking fullback makes this
play a sure 5 yard gainer each time it is run.

One more play makes our tailback series complete. That is
the option play to the weak side. We used to call the play a 49
belly, where we faked to the fullback and made the option on the
defensive end. However, since adding the 41 option to our offensive attack, we have changed and also made the 49 option a triple
option. If your quarterback is capable of making the correct

reads, then we suggest that you use the triple option technique. If the quarterback is not capable of making the correct reads then we merely fake to the fullback, block the defensive tackle with our 7 tackle and option the defensive end. This type of option is actually giving us an outside belly option to the weak side. We will give you the triple option technique first and the belly option technique last.

Play Call: Right or Left 49 Option (Diagrams 5-20 and 5-21)

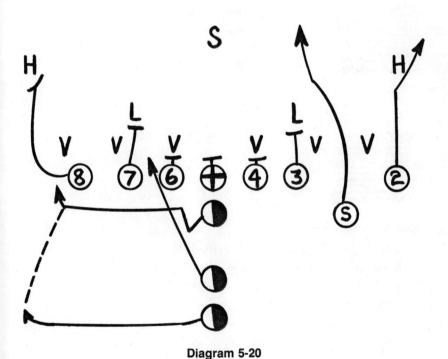

Diagram 5-20

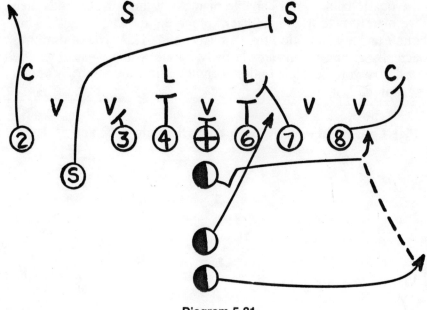

Diagram 5-21

Blocking Rules for 49 Option

2 End—run 100 pattern at your halfback

3 Tackle—gap, over, linebacker *Goo*

4 Guard—gap, over, linebacker *Goo*

5 Center—over, weak-side gap, fill area ON-OVER - N.S.

6 Guard—gap, over, linebacker *Goo*

7 Tackle—gap, linebacker inside *Goo*

8 End—release outside and block your halfback *Goo*

Slotback—block safety or run a pattern down the middle

Fullback—run at outside hip of 6 guard, possible ball carrier so put a soft
    squeeze on the ball

Tailback—run lateral to the sideline looking for possible pitch from the quarterback. If quarterback turns upfield, maintain pitch relationship with him

Quarterback—step at 45 degrees to fullback, reading the defensive tackle, give to fullback if defensive tackle is staying at home or going outside. Otherwise keep and option the defensive end as in a 41 option technique

Coaching Points: Quarterback, fullback, and tailback action are the same as in the 41 option. We use the same drills to perfect the 49 option that we used to develop the 41 option. These drills were explained in detail following the 41 option play earlier in this chapter (Diagrams 5-7 through 5-10). The 6 guard must constantly be reminded and checked to see that he is always taking the same 2-foot split on every offensive play so that the fullback and quarterback maintain the same relationship on every option play.

If our quarterbacks are having trouble reading both the defensive tackle and the defensive end, then we make the play a belly option instead of a triple option. We have the 7 tackle block, gap, over, linebacker; leaving only one person for the quarterback to option—the defensive end. The 8 end would also have to block gap, over, linebacker, for us to run the belly option. Diagrams 5-22 and 5-23 will show how we block the belly option.

Before leaving the tailback plays from the Slot I offense, we think that you can see the many more possiblities as far as running plays and blocking combinations are concerned. However, over the past few years we have dropped plays because we were not getting the yardage that makes teaching another play and more blocking rules worthwhile. Our philosophy has been that if a play is not working successfully over a period of time then get rid of it and save practice time. In other words, we do not believe in cluttering the offense just so you can have 20 to 30 running plays to each side. Keep the plays as simple as possible and use only the successful ones. We do not recommend keeping both the 41 belly and the 41 option or the 49 belly and the 49 option in your offensive attack. Use only the option that your quarterbacks are able to execute properly.

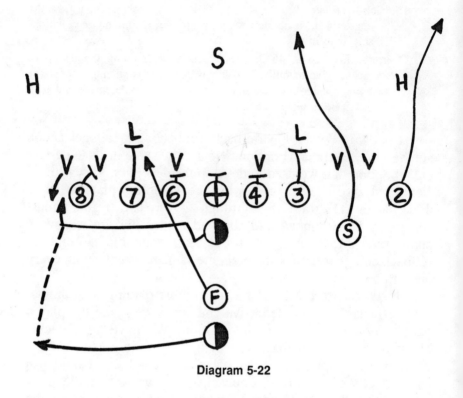

Diagram 5-22

STANCE OF THE TAILBACK

One important item that should be mentioned here is the stance that our tailbacks use. We have our tailbacks use a 2-point, upright stance. We like this particular stance because it allows our primary running back—the tailback—to be able to see the defensive personnel and alignments.

In the 2-point stance, the tailback's body is bent slightly forward at the waist with his hands resting slightly above the knees. His head is up with the eyes looking straight ahead. The knees should be slightly bent and the feet should be spread ap-

49 Belly

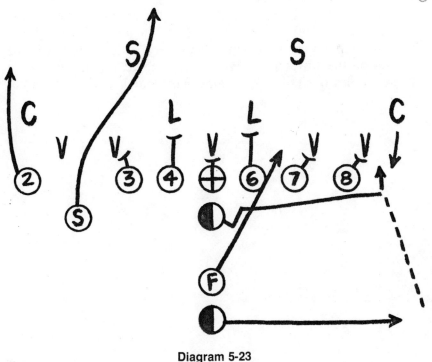

Diagram 5-23

proximately shoulder-width apart. The feet should be in a parallel position in order to allow the tailback to start in either direction with a certain degree of quickness. Both feet should be flat
on the ground with the majority of the weight on the balls of the
feet.

We have a theory about the placement of the hands on the
knees in the 2-point, upright stance. It is natural to place the
thumbs on the inside of the knees with the fingers on the outside
of the legs. By doing this, we feel that the individual will place
too much weight on the legs thus making it more difficult to start
quickly because the weight must first be shifted from the legs by

lifting the arms before the individual may start in either direction. Therefore, we have our tailbacks place the thumb on the outside of the leg and the fingers on the inside of the legs or knee. This is a somewhat awkward position and very little weight can be placed on the lower legs. We believe, however, that this little trick enables our tailbacks to start more quickly in either direction.

6

Fullback Plays for the Slot I Offense

The fullback offense in our Slot I offensive attack consists of only five basic running plays not counting the possibilities of his getting the ball on the 41 option or the 49 option. If you are using these two triple option plays, 41 option and 49 option, then the fullback can carry the ball on seven plays in the Slot I offense. Of these seven plays, two are trap plays, three are quick-hitting plays with one-on-one blocking, and, of course, two are the results of the triple option plays that are included in the offensive attack.

Before getting into the fullback plays, let's consider the type of individuals that we look for when selecting fullbacks for the offense. As we mentioned earlier, when selecting our fullback candidates we basically look for only two traits. They are (1) physical strength, and (2) a strong desire to hit people. A good fullback must have these two traits in order for him to carry out his responsibilities in the Slot I offense.

We feel that our fullback candidates must have above average physical strength in order to carry out his primary responsibility in the offense, that is blocking ahead of our tailback. On many of our offensive plays, the fullback is responsible for blocking the defensive end out or for lead-blocking through a hole on the linebacker. If he is going to block defensive ends and linebackers, then he will, indeed, have to be a very strong individual physically.

Notice that we have said nothing about the size of the fullback. We feel that size is not very important if the fullback has the physical strength to block the defensive people that we ask him to block. Of course, the more size that the fullback has, probably the better all-around football player he will be. Just to give you an idea of the size of most of our fullbacks, they have ranged from the smallest at 155 pounds to the largest at 185 pounds.

The second quality that we mentioned was the desire to hit. We feel that in order for the fullback to do a good job offensively he must be either blocking or being tackled on every offensive play. If he is going to be either hit or hitting someone else on every offensive play, then he must have a love for contact. We often overlook the fact that a good fullback is getting tackled on every play that he fakes. If he is not getting tackled when he is faking, then we had better do one of two things; either give him the football or find a new fullback to fake to because he is not doing his job.

Another quality that a good fullback must have is the ability to carry the football on the short trapping game or the quick-hitting, inside running game. He must be somewhat of a threat to the defense on the inside if the triple option, sweep, etc. are going to work on the outside with the tailback carrying the football.

Again, when selecting the fullback look for the two qualities of physical strength and a desire to hit. If your fullback has these two things, you can definitely make him a fine blocker, as well as a fine ball carrier for the inside running game.

STANCE OF THE FULLBACK

When considering a stance for your fullback, we feel that any stance that will allow him to get his assignment done in a proper manner should be allowed. One can find approximately as many coaches having their fullbacks using the 2-point, upright stance as are having the fullbacks use a 3- or 4-point stance.

The coaches using the 2-point, upright stance for their fullbacks will argue that the upright stance helps give their offensive attack a certain degree of added deception. It is not quite as easy for the defense people to see the tailback if the fullback is in a

2-point, upright stance in front of him. Another reason that many coaches prefer the upright stance is that it allows the fullback to see the defensive personnel and alignments. They feel that this makes it easier to influence a defensive player to go with the fake of the fullback.

Now let's consider the 3- and 4-point stance for the full-backs. We start every one of our fullbacks in a 3-point stance but if we find that they are pointing in one direction or another we will put the other hand on the ground thus giving us a 4-point stance. We will use the 3- or 4-point stance instead of the 2-point stance because we feel that it allows the fullback to explode on the snap of the ball toward the line of scrimmage.

In the 3-point stance, the feet should be about shoulder-width apart and not staggered more than toe to heel. We strive for a parallel stance but find that most fullbacks will stagger the feet slightly. We will not allow a very large stagger because then the fullbacks cannot move laterally or forward equally well. The weight should be on the balls of the feet with the toes pointed straight ahead.

The hand that is placed down on the ground should be in a position under the eyes and slightly inside the knee. The elbow should be locked straight so that more weight can be shifted forward on the down hand. The fingers of the down hand should be flexed in order to form a base of support. The other arm should be rested on the thigh of that leg. The arm should be bent and positioned just above the knee.

The knees should be bent at an angle that will keep the buttocks and hips high. The player's back should be straight and almost parallel to the ground. The head should be up and the eyes should be focused on the linemen ahead.

Again, if the fullback is pointing in the direction of the down hand have him put the other hand on the ground also. This will tend to balance the shoulders and keep them parallel to the ground. One word of caution—do not let the fullbacks place too much weight forward on the down hand or hands.

We would now like to give you the fullback offensive plays using the same format that we used with the tailback plays. The right formation diagrammed against a wide tackle 6-2 defense and the left formation diagrammed against the Oklahoma 5-4-2 defense.

Play Call: Right or Left 32 (Diagrams 6-1 and 6-2)

Blocking Rules for 32

2 End—first man inside

3 Tackle—gap, over, outside *Goo*

4 Guard—gap, over, fill area *Goo*

5 Center—strong-side gap, over, fill area *GN-oUER - S.S. GAPS*

6 Guard—gap, over, fill area *Goo*

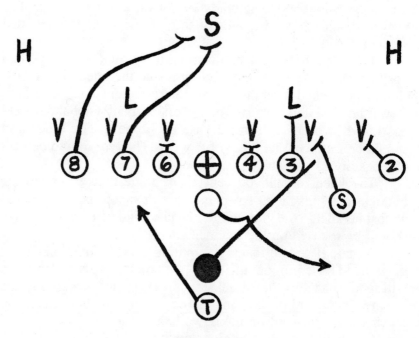

Diagram 6-1

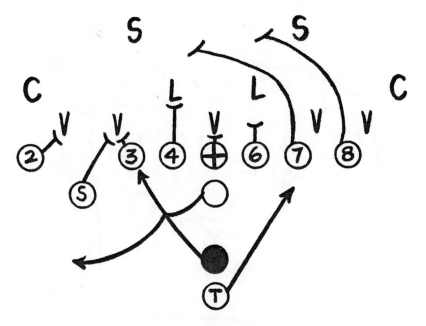

Diagram 6-2

7 Tackle—release inside for halfback or safety

8 End—release inside for halfback or safety

Slotback—gap, man on, double-team with 3 tackle   *GAP, ON, OUER, INSIDE*

Fullback—slant at outside hip of 3 tackle

Tailback—dive at 7 hole

Quarterback—step out and hand to fullback, continue on as if to set up to pass

Coaching Points: This is a very simple play but has been quite a successful one to run at people keying and going with the tailback. The line is one-on-one blocking with a double team in the 3 tackle area against most defenses. We teach our linemen to put the hat right on the numbers and drive the defensive people backward as far as possible. This is a very quick-hitting play and

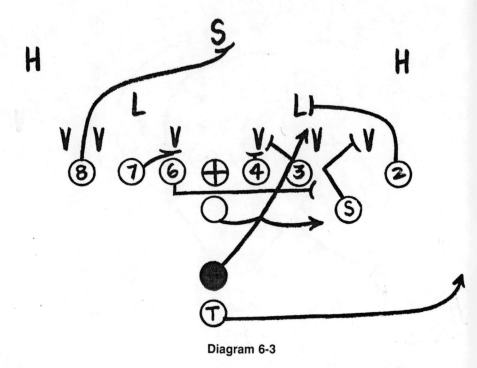

Diagram 6-3

does not give the defense much time to react before the fullback
has gained 3 to 5 yards. We like to run this from a white formation (8 end split) because the defense usually makes a slight
adjustment with their linebackers or secondary. We hope to gain
only 3 to 5 yards each time that we run this play but it has broken
for some long gainers.

This next play is the bread and butter play in the fullback's
series. The 33 must be a very successful play if the tailback series
is going to be worth the paper that it is printed on. If we cannot
run the 33 then our entire offense is going to be somewhat
stymied for the afternoon. We have run this play as the only
fullback play on many an afternoon.

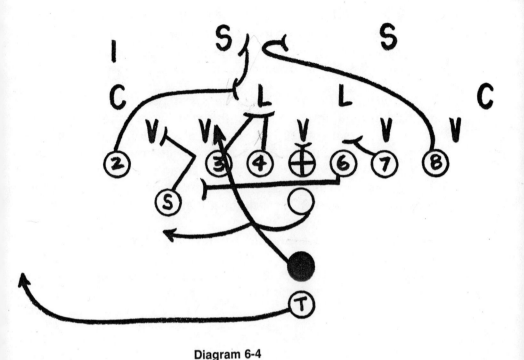

Diagram 6-4

Play Call: Right or Left 33 (Diagrams 6-3 and 6-4)

Blocking Rules for 33

2 End—Linebacker inside, if split block your̶ halfback *SS.*
3 Tackle—gap, drive man on 4 guard, first man inside *GAP, INSIDE*
4 Guard—gap, post man over, drive block man on 5, linebacker inside *GAP-ON-OVER INSIDE*
5 Center—over, first man away *ON-OVER-WIS,*
6 Guard—pull and trap first man past 3 tackle
7 Tackle—pull and seal for 6 guard *INSIDE FOR 6, GUARD*
8 End—safety or opposite halfback *or S.B. W.S*
Slotback—fake block at man on or outside 3 tackle, then block first man
    outside *IF 2 END IS SPLIT LB INSIDE*

Fullback—ball carrier, stay as close to double-team block as possible

Tailback—run as in a 41, try to get downfield but do not cut the arc short

Quarterback—reverse pivot, hand to fullback, continue out, hiding your
passing hand from the outside defensive personnel

Coaching Points: This is the most important play in our fullback's running game. From this play we set up most of our sprint out passing attack, we run our belly option from it, and we keep the opponent's defense from keying too heavily on the tailback. We expect this particular play to gain at least 5 yards per try on the average, and have on many occasions broken the play for a long gainer or touchdown. On many afternoons, the 33 is the only play that we run from our fullback series.

If the 2 end is split, then we have the slotback block inside on the linebacker as is shown in Diagram 6-5. The 2 end, in the same diagram then goes downfield and either blocks the defensive halfback or runs the halfback deep on a pass route.

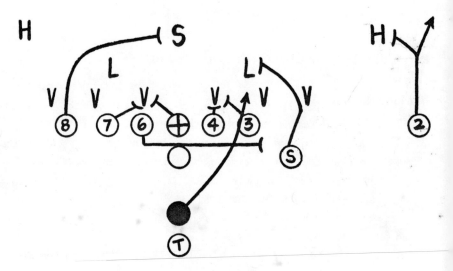

Diagram 6-5

The double-team block by the 3 tackle and the 4 guard is a very important block because it allows the fullback a rather wide alley in which to run. If people play the defensive guard slightly inside our 4 guard, then we allow the 3 tackle to block on the linebacker creating a double-team block in that area. We always get the double-team block, but it is sometimes between 3 tackle and 2 end, 3 tackle and slotback, or 3 tackle and 4 guard.

The 6 guard and 7 tackle use the same technique to pull and pull and seal respectively. We teach our linemen to pull by taking a short step with the lead foot in the direction they are pulling. Then pivot and move down the line. Thus, if the 6 guard was to pull right, he would take a short step with the right foot, sideways or to the right. Then pivot bringing the left past the right and moving down the line of scrimmage toward the trap block. We always want his head in the hole so the defensive person must fight through the head and shoulders to get to the ball carrier.

The 7 tackle uses the same pulling technique as the 6 guard to pull and seal for the 6 guard. What he is really doing is trapping or cutting off the player in the 6 guard area. This sealing technique is very important and should constantly be checked to make sure the 7 tackle is sealing the area. If the defensive people are blowing through the guard center area, they can catch the fullback from behind and give you a poor play.

We have the quarterback use the reverse pivot technique for a couple of reasons. First, it gets the quarterback out of the way of the pulling 6 guard. If he reverse pivots, it takes him away from the line of scrimmage allowing the 6 guard to pull with no one in his pulling lane.

Another reason we use the reverse pivot is that it then makes the defense decide whether the fullback is getting the ball or whether the quarterback is going to pitch as in a 41 or whether the play will end up as a belly option or a sprint out pass. This split second indecision on the part of the defense allows us to get the blocking angles that we would like to have for a successful play.

The tailback should run a 41 or 41 belly route making the defense decide if he is going to get the ball. We would like the tailback to get downfield and block but do not want him to cut his route up short in order to get downfield. If the defense does not respect the tailback, then we will come with the 41 belly or the 41 option and put pressure on the defensive corner.

Again, the 33 is the bread and butter play of the fullback series. If it is run properly, it will put enough pressure on the defense to allow the tailback to run almost wild. You must make the 33 work early in the game if you are to have a successful afternoon running or passing.

Play Call: Right or Left 34 (Diagrams 6-6 and 6-7)

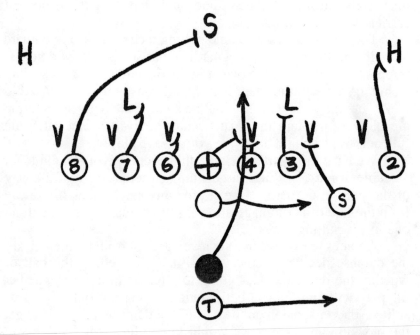

Diagram 6-6

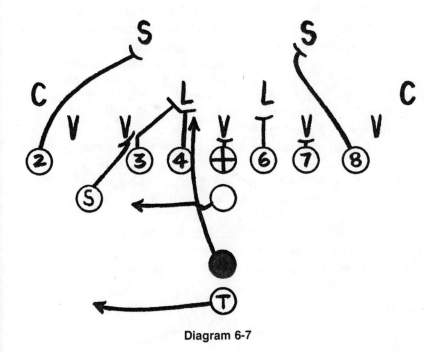

Diagram 6-7

Blocking Rules for 34

2 End—safety or your halfback
3 Tackle—gap, over, linebacker
4 Guard—gap, over, linebacker
5 Center—strong-side gap, over
6 Guard—gap, over, linebacker
7 Tackle—gap, over, linebacker
8 End—safety or your halfback
Slotback—cut off man on outside of 3 tackle
Fullback—ball carrier, run at inside hip of 4 guard, cut to daylight
Tailback—fake as in a 41 or 41 option
Quarterback—step short, hand to fullback, continue out as in 41 option

Coaching Points: This is our isolation play to our fullback. The play is the fastest hitting play in our offensive attack and is one of the basic short yardage and goal line plays. The line blocking is one-on-one except in the 4 guard area and we would like to have a double-team block either with the 4 guard and center or the 4 guard and the 3 tackle. We school our fullbacks so that they know where the double-team block will be and allow them to cut to daylight.

The quarterback should merely turn to the strong side and hand to the fullback. Time will not allow any fancy footwork or reverse pivots by the quarterback. Do not allow the quarterback to step too far to the strong side and get in the way of the fullback.

The next play is a very quick trap to the fullback. After the defense adjusts to our options or to the 33, or at least becomes very conscious of them, we come back with our 35. We feel that

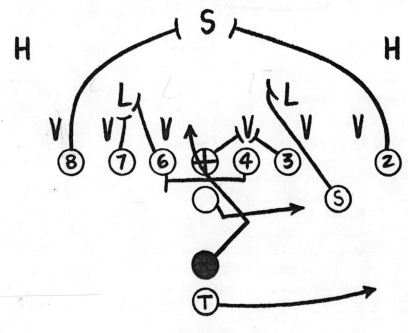

Diagram 6-8

this is an excellent way to combat this adjustment by the defense—with a quick trap into the center of the line behind the pursuing linebackers.

Play Call: Right or Left 35: Diagrams 6-8 and 6-9)

Blocking Rules for 35

    2 End—safety or your halfback

    3 Tackle—first man inside

    4 Guard—pull and trap first man past 5 center

    5 Center—over, strong-side gap ON = OVER = SS. GAP

    6 Guard—drive block man on 5 center, linebacker outside INSIDE - LB OUTSIDE

    7 Tackle—gap, over, linebacker inside

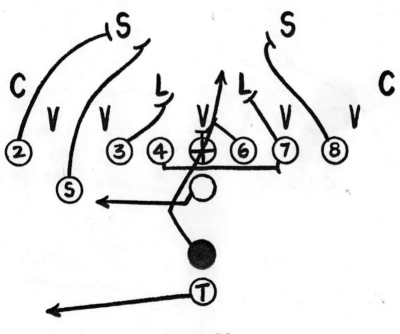

Diagram 6-9

8 End—safety or your halfback
Slotback—release inside and block in middle third or safety
Fullback—start as in 34, then break back to weak side, ball carrier
Tailback—run a 41 option or 41 belly route
Quarterback—step back and give to fullback, then fake a 41 option or 41
    belly action

Coaching Points: The backfield action should resemble the 34 and the 41 option as closely as possible. The quarterback should open almost straight back in order to allow the fullback to clear and to get out of the way of the pulling guard. The tailback should go wide to the strong side as in a 41 option or as he does in the 34. The fullback lead-steps as in the 34 toward the inside leg of the 4 guard. After the first step, he should break back toward the weak side, following the pulling 4 guard.

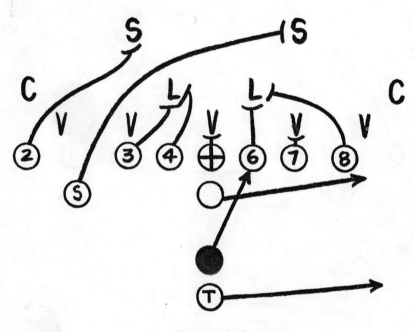

Diagram 6-10

Quickness is the key to a well executed 35. The fullback must hit as quickly as possible behind the 4 guard. The fullback should be schooled to the fact that against an odd-front defense, he will have to break outside toward the 8 end and against an even-front defense the break should be almost up the middle and possibly slightly toward the 4 guard area.

The pulling 4 guard is taught the same technique that we teach the 6 guard. We explained this technique earlier in the chapter and we teach the technique to all our offensive linemen from 3 tackle to 7 tackle.

The final play in our fullback's series is the isolation play to the weak side or the 8 end side of the offense. This play is the same as the 34 only to the weak side of center so it becomes a 36.

Play Call: Right or Left 36 (Diagrams 6-10 and 6-11)

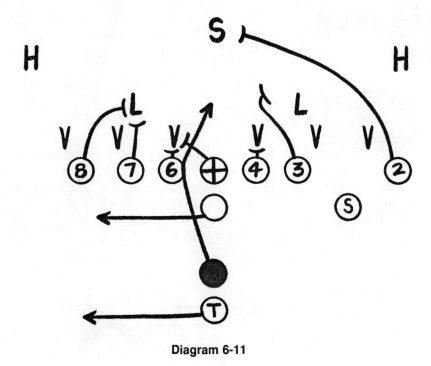

Diagram 6-11

Blocking Rules for 36

2 End—safety or opposite halfback

3 Tackle—release inside and block downfield

4 Guard—gap, over, linebacker

5 Center—over, strong-side linebacker

6 Guard—gap, over, linebacker

7 Tackle—gap, over, linebacker

8 End—gap, over, linebacker

Slotback—release downfield on safety or opposite halfback

Fullback—ball carrier, run at inside hip of 6 guard and cut off the double team block

Tailback—fake a 49 option route

Quarterback—step, hand to fullback, continue out and fake a 49 option

Coaching Points: The coaching points are the same as for the 34. This play, like the 34, is a very fast-hitting play. The quarterback should merely turn to the weak side and hand to the fullback. Do not allow the quarterback to take too long a step or he will be in the fullback's path into the line.

This completes our fullback offense except for the possibility of his getting the ball on a 41 or a 49 option. Before leaving the fullback offense, we should take a look at the technique required of the fullback in the 41 or 49 options.

The quarterback-fullback action is basically the same as the much publicized Texas Wishbone attack. The fullback is three yards behind the line of scrimmage, or approximately one yard behind the quarterback, in a 3- or 4-point stance. On the snap count, he should step and drive at the outside hip of the guard. He should form a pocket for the ball by raising the inside elbow and placing his outside hand, palm up, about waist high on the inside hip.

The fullback is responsible for the handoff so he should look for the football and actually run into it. He should put a soft squeeze on the ball and not cover it completely until the quarterback releases the ball.

The three checkpoints as far as the coach is concerned are: (1) make sure the fullback is always running the same path at the outside hip of the guard, don't allow him to belly or round his route; (2) whether or not you get the ball, always make a good fake and drive anyone in the area backwards; (3) upon entering the seam, always go outside or behind the tackle's block.

Although the fullback does not carry the ball as often as the tailback, we know that without some degree of success with the fullback's running offense our team offense will have a very difficult afternoon.

7

Coaching Slotback Plays

Our slotback provides the offense with the versatility needed in a good offensive attack. The slotback gives us the necessary counter and reverses to keep the defense honest while also providing for a quick receiver in our passing attack. Although the slotback carries the ball very seldom, the three offensive plays that he carries the ball are very important to the Slot I running attack.

Before getting into the slotback's running plays, let's first examine the slotback's qualifications and stance. The actual positioning of the slotback makes him somewhat of a unique person. He is always a yard behind and a yard outside of the 3 tackle. In this position, he must be a blocker, runner, and a pass receiver. As we mentioned earlier, when selecting personnel for our offense we consider first the thing that he will do most often. Therefore, we consider our slotback as a blocker first, a runner second, and a pass receiver last. The ideal slotback would be a combination of the fullback and the 2 end. The slotback will do a great amount of double-team blocking with the 3 tackle, and therefore must have the physical strength to complete a good double-team block successfully. He must have a certain amount of quickness in order to complete the double-team block before the defensive man gets past the 3 tackle. He must possess a love for contact because what he will be doing most of the time is contacting the defensive tackle.

When considering the slotback as a runner, we look for speed and quickness. He will be carrying the ball on counters and reverses and, therefore, will not need the overpowering strength of a fullback. We are trying to fool people when the slotback carries the football and the slotback does not need the strength to run over people. Naturally, the more strength that he has the better blocker and ball carrier he probably will be.

Finally, as a pass receiver, the slotback should possess speed and quickness along with a good set of hands. He must be able to complete a good pass route quickly and then be able to catch the football if it is thrown to him. We do complete many passes to our slotback, so he then will use his knowledge of running to move the football further down the field.

STANCE OF THE SLOTBACK

Since our slotback always lines up a yard behind and a yard outside the 3 tackle, we have him use a 3-point stance. From the 3-point stance, we feel that he will be quicker in firing out for his blocking assignment, pulling on a counter or reverse, and finally, in releasing downfield on a pass pattern.

In the 3-point stance, the feet should be shoulder-width apart and not staggered more than toe to heel. We strive for a parallel stance but often find that most slotbacks will stagger their feet slightly. We will not allow the slotback to stagger his feet very much because then he will not be able to move laterally very well. The weight should be on the balls of the feet with the toes pointed straight ahead.

The hand that is placed down on the ground should be in a position under the eyes and slightly inside the knee. The elbow should be locked straight so that more weight can be shifted forward on the down hand. The fingers of the down hand should be flexed in order to form a base of support. The other arm should be rested on the thigh of that leg. The arm should be bent and positioned slightly above the knee.

The knees should be bent at an angle that will keep the buttocks and hips high. The player's back should be straight and almost parallel to the gound. The head should be up with the eyes focused on the defensive person ahead.

Many coaches will argue that the wingback or slotback should be in a 2-point upright stance but because we think of our slotback as a blocker first we want him in a stance that will allow him to carry out the primary responsibility properly. We would not dream of putting our linemen in a 2-point stance so we likewise put the slotback and the linemen in a 3-point stance. We have on rare occasion allowed the slotback to use a 4-point stance similar to the fullback's. The important consideration is whether or not he is getting his assignments carried out properly, not so much the stance that he is using.

Play Call: Right or Left 17 (Diagrams 7-1 and 7-2)

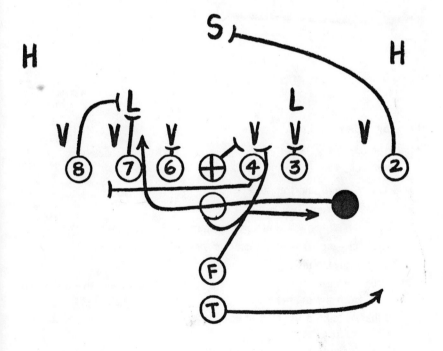

Diagram 7-1

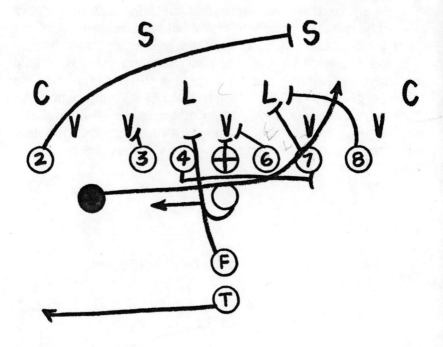

Diagram 7-2

Blocking Rules for 17

    2 End—release downfield for safety or opposite halfback

    3 Tackle—gap, over, slightly outside

    4 Guard—pull and trap at 7

    5 Center—strong-side gap, fill area

    6 Guard—gap, over, double team man on 5

    7 Tackle—gap, first man inside on or off the line

    8 End—release inside for linebacker

    Slotback—ball carrier, pull toward weak side and take inside handoff
        from the quarterback

    Fullback—fake a tight 33 at outside hip of 4 guard and help fill for 4
        guard

    Tailback—fake a 41 option

Quarterback—reverse pivot, fake a 33 to fullback, hand inside to the
slotback, continue out as in a 41 option.

Coaching Points: Notice that we again have the 4 guard
pulling and trapping. The pulling technique is the same as the 6
guard's technique that we explained earlier. Also, we do teach
the pulling technique to all of our interior linemen because not
only do the 4 and 6 guards pull, but the 3 and 7 tackles must pull
and seal for the guards. The technique is always the same for all
pulling linemen. That is take a short lead step in the direction you
are pulling, then pivot and move down the line of scrimmage in
the pulling direction.

The backfield techniques are very simple because the backs,
other than the slotback, run patterns that they have already
learned. The fullback merely runs a 33 but must be aware of the
fact that he must seal for the pulling 4 guard. If your play se-
quence has been developed properly, the fake of the 33 should
help set up the fullback's block. The tailback merely runs a 41
option or 41 belly route depending upon which one you have in
your offensive play series. The quarterback must reverse pivot
and fake a 33 to the fullback. After the fullback has cleared, he
should hand inside to the slotback coming down the line of
scrimmage. It is important for the quarterback to reverse pivot to
allow the pulling guard to get by. The reverse pivot technique
should take the quarterback away from the line of scrimmage far
enough to allow the 4 guard to pass by and also to allow the
slotback to go between the quarterback and the line of scrimmage. The quarterback should carry out the 41 option or 41 belly
fake with the tailback.

The slotback should actually use a technique similar to the
pulling guards to get started down the line of scrimmage. For
example, if a right 17 has been called, the slotback should take a
short step with his left foot, pivot on the left foot and come down
the line of scrimmage with the right foot. The left arm should be
up across the chest and the right arm down about waist high
forming a pocket for the quarterback to put the ball. The slotback
should follow the 4 guard and cut upfield at the first spot that
opens in the defensive front.

Play Call: Right or Left 18 (Diagrams 7-3 and 7-4)

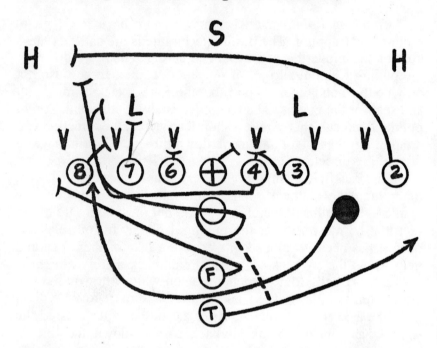

Diagram 7-3

Blocking Rules for 18

2 End—safety or ~~opposite~~ halfback   *w S.   H.B.*

3 Tackle—pull and seal for 4 guard   *SEAL INSIDE FOR 4 GUARD*

4 Guard—pull to weak side and lead up the hole, look to the inside

5 Center—over, strong-side gap, fill area   *ON - OVER - SS. GAP*

6 Guard—gap, over, post block if 7 tackle is free, 7 tackle is covered, fill area   *GOOD*

7 Tackle—gap, post man over or slightly outside, drive block first man to the inside   *GOOD INSIDE*

8 End—gap, over, drive block man on 7 tackle, no man on 7 tackle block linebacker inside   *GAP—ON - OVER - INSIDE*

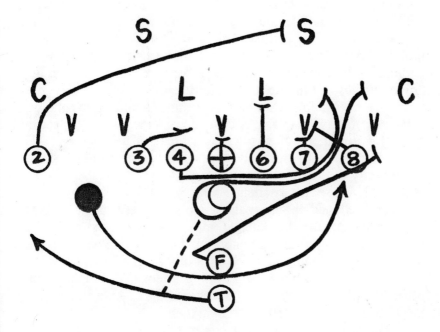

Diagram 7-4

Slotback—ball carrier, pivot deep on a route between fullback and tailback, take inside handoff from the tailback and follow the fullback

Fullback—head fake and jab step to the strong side, then block on first man past the 8 end

Tailback—receive ball as in a 41, then hand to the slotback inside, continue out as on a 41

Quarterback—reverse pivot and pitch to the tailback as in a 41, then complete your spin and lead through the hole behind the 4 guard and fullback

Coaching Points: The line techniques are much the same as in the 17 except that the 4 guard now leads upfield instead of trapping at the hole. Usually there will be a double-team block in the vicinity of the 7 tackle, depending upon the defense, and the 4 guard cuts upfield just past the double-team block. He should look to the inside and block any pursuing linemen or linebackers coming to the football. If no one is coming, have him continue downfield toward the defensive halfback.

The backfield techniques are rather simple but timing is very important. The quarterback again reverse pivots to clear the pulling 4 guard. He then pitches the ball as he does on a 41, makes the complete spin, and blocks through the hole. He should run directly at the defensive halfback once through the hole and block only those that challenge him.

The fullback should make a jab step and head fake to the strong side making the defense think that a 41 is coming, then come back to the weak side and kick the defensive end or corner out creating a running lane for the slotback. This fullback block is much like a trap block by a pulling lineman. His head should be in the hole forcing the end or corner to the outside and creating the running lane inside the defensive end.

The tailback has a new technique but it is a simple one to carry out. He takes the pitch as in a 41 then hands inside to the slotback, making sure of a good handoff to the slotback. He then continues out as if he is running a 41. A good fake after the hand off will freeze the linebackers and secondary long enough to allow our offensive personnel to have the good angle on their blocking assignments. This play is very effective if the offense has been running the 41 successfully.

The slotback pivots deep and runs a route that will take him right inside the tailback. He takes an inside handoff from the tailback then follows the blockers ahead of him through the hole. The running lane should open up just outside the 8 end and just inside the fullback's block on the defensive end or corner. The outside arm should be up and the inside arm down forming the pocket for the tailback to put the ball.

We like to run this play with our 2 end split, especially if the defense is rotating their secondary or spreading the defense to the split side. This adjustment allows us a sizable gain before the defense can react to the ball.

The last play in our slotback's running series is a variety of the triple option using the fullback, quarterback, and the slotback. We normally put the slotback in motion to get a proper relationship with the fullback and tailback. The tailback now becomes the lead blocker and the slotback the option or pitch man. The quarterback can either hand to the fullback as on a 36, keep the ball and turn upfield, or pitch to the slotback.

Play Call: Right or Left 19 (Diagrams 7-5 and 7-6)

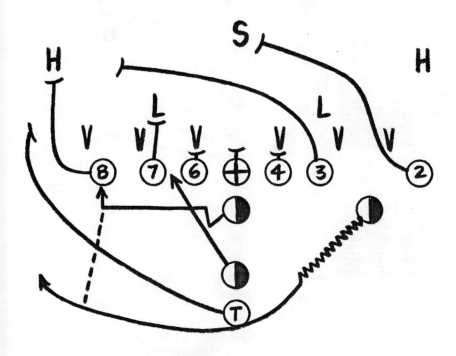

Diagram 7-5

Blocking Rules for 19

 2 End—release inside for safety or opposite halfback, if split run a streak pattern driving the halfback deep

 3 Tackle—gap, over, release inside for safety or halfback

 4 Guard—gap, over, fill area

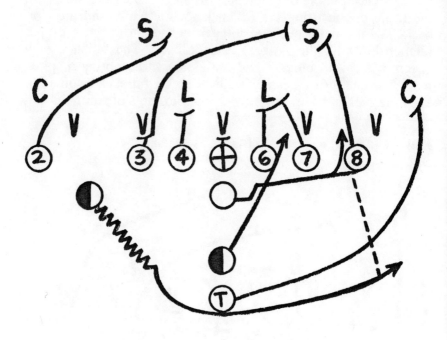

Diagram 7-6

5 Center—weak-side gap, over, fill area

6 Guard—gap, over, drive block man on 5

7 Tackle—gap, linebacker inside

8 End—release across defensive end and block your halfback, if split, run a streak pattern driving the halfback deep

Slotback—Possible ball carrier, run pitch route and maintain good relationship with the fullback

Fullback—run 49 option route, soft squeeze on the ball, possible ball carrier

Tailback—release outside and block the defensive man responsible for the outside one-third

Quarterback—run a 49 option, reading the defensive tackle and end if pitching look to the slotback.

Coaching Points: All assignments for the 19 are the same as they were on the 49 option for everyone but the tailback and the slotback. On the 19, the slotback instead of the tailback becomes the pitch man, and for the first time, the tailback is not the pitch man but the lead blocker. We have found that this option really confuses the defensive people who are responsible for the pitch man. They have in most cases been taught that the pitch man will be the tailback and suddenly the tailback is blocking them and the slotback is the pitch man.

This play can be very effective from any of the split formations red, white or blue, because the interior blocking is not necessary. The split ends help tell the offense who is responsible deep, who has containment, etc.

Before leaving the slotback series, remember that even though the slotback can carry the ball on 6 plays (three to each side) the slotback series does complement the rest of the offense and is a necessary component. It will help keep the defense from keying too heavily upon the tailback and the fullback if a good counter can be run. It provides balance to the offense by presenting some counters and reverses to the defensive personnel. Timing of the slotback's series is very important and should be checked and rechecked. In teaching three plays, only two blocking rules must be learned because the other play, the 19, uses the same rules as the 49 option.

8

Coaching the Slot I Quarterback

Before getting into the quarterback's running plays, we should review the qualifications and characteristics that we like our quarterbacks to possess. The single most important quality of a good quarterback is leadership. He is the coach on the playing field and therefore must be the team leader or at least one of its leaders. He must possess a strong, commanding voice that will make him a forceful and respected team leader. He must be a team leader both on and off the football field. Our coaching staff looks for the individual who is capable of making things happen on and off the football field. As the playing field coach, the quarterback must be a person who can make the team move the ball and score. He must always be a confident leader and, in order to possess this confidence, he must have enough intelligence to understand the entire offensive system. He must have a certain degree of poise and common football sense to be able to lead the team down the field by selecting the correct play at the right moment.

Courage is another important trait that the quarterback must have. We believe that all football players have a certain amount of courage but the quarterback, as the field leader, must have the courage to stand up for his teammates, to stand behind the play that he has called regardless of the outcome, and the courage to follow the game plan to the end.

Now let's consider the qualities of a good quarterback from the physical standpoint. Physically, the quarterback must be a good ball handler who has quick hands and feet, and he must possess a certain amount of speed to be able consistently to execute all the offensive plays. He must be physically able to run the football as well as strong enough to throw it accurately. From the physical standpoint, size is not nearly as important as one might think. We have had three outstanding quarterbacks all under 5'7" and 140 pounds. We do feel that if you have people of equal ability and leadership that the taller of the two quarterbacks will probably be the better quarterback. This is because he is in a better position to see the opponent's defensive personnel over your offensive line.

QUARTERBACK'S STANCE

There are a number of ways of putting the quarterback in a stance behind the center, so we will give you the method that we teach each of our quarterbacks. We want them to be very comfortable in their stance. Their feet should be about shoulder-width apart in a parallel or slightly staggered stance. We never allow our quarterbacks to stagger more than toe to instep. The weight should be on the balls of the feet. The knees should be slightly bent depending upon the height of the quarterback and also the height of the offensive center. Above all else, the quarterback should be comfortable and relaxed in his stance.

The hand placement of the quarterback is very important and we teach the same hand placement to all our quarterbacks. The right hand should be on top regardless of whether the quarterback is right or left handed. He should place the right hand under the center's crotch, slightly deeper than the wrist. The top hand, the right hand, should apply a certain amount of upward pressure so that the center can feel a target at which he is to snap the ball. The thumbs should be placed together with the right hand palm facing the ground and the left hand palm facing the sky. Some coaches will require the left hand to be slightly forward so the first joint of the right hand fits into the left hand thumb's groove just above the first joint. We do not stress this to our quarterbacks because they will find the position that is most comfortable to them anyway. We do want the left hand and fingers facing somewhat downward to serve as a stop for the ball.

We never want the quarterback to allow the center to snap the ball completely through his hands.

The fingers should be slightly curled on both hands to allow the quarterback to grasp the football on the snap. Make sure the quarterback receives the ball with the laces in the proper position so he will be ready to throw the ball without unnecessary ball handling.

Many coaches commit what we consider a cardinal sin and that is leaving it up to the quarterbacks and centers to work together on the snap before and after practice on their own. As we mentioned earlier, during the option drills we always take some time, daily, to work on the center-quarterback exchange. Every offensive play starts with the exchanged ball and, therefore, time must be taken to insure a correctly executed exchange.

QUARTERBACK'S FOOTWORK

Since incorporating the triple option technique into our offensive attack, we have to teach our quarterbacks two types of footwork: reverse pivot and open step.

On the reverse pivot, the quarterback must execute a three-quarter pivot as soon as he receives the ball from the center. Thus, if the play called was a Right 41, the quarterback would pivot on the right foot and swing the left foot in an approximately three-quarter turn (Diagram 8-1). The quarterback should then step with the pivot foot making the proper pitch or handoff required for the play called (Diagram 8-2).

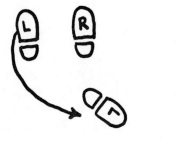

Diagram 8-1

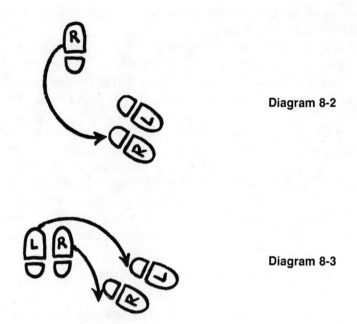

Diagram 8-2

Diagram 8-3

The open step technique is required on the 41 and 49 options and should be executed as follows; The quarterback should step at about a 45 degree angle away from the line of scrimmage with the lead foot. He should then bring the trail foot up alongside the lead foot and make the correct mesh with the fullback. If a Right 41 Option were called, the quarterback's footwork would be as follows (Diagram 8-3): He would lead-step at 45 degrees with the right foot and then bring the left foot up alongside the right foot making the mesh with the fullback.

QUARTERBACK'S HANDOFFS

Our quarterbacks must also learn two handoff techniques: the pitch and the straight handoff. On the pitch technique, whether from a reverse pivot as on a 41 or from an option technique as on a 41 option, we tell our quarterbacks that they are responsible for a good pitch. The pitch should hit the tailback somewhere between the shoulders and the waist. The pitch on a 41 should be a two-handed pitch as the quarterback completes the reverse pivot. It should be slightly ahead of the tailback because he is moving toward the sideline. This is a very easy technique to teach. Just have the quarterbacks reverse pivot and toss the ball to a manager, coach, fellow player, as he completes the pivot. He will quite naturally pitch with both hands as he completes the reverse pivot.

The option pitch can be made with either a one-or two-handed pitch. We start all quarterbacks with a two-handed pitch but if they can pitch one-handed to our satisfaction, then we allow them to use the one-handed pitch. On the two-handed pitch, we have the quarterbacks carry the ball about chest high in both hands. The pitch is made, similar to a chest pass in basketball, by extending the arms in the direction of the pitch and letting go of the ball. We drill on this pitch daily also as part of our option drills diagrammed in Chapter 5.

On the straight handoff, the quarterback is responsible for placing the ball in the pocket formed by the ball carrier. When taking a handoff, we ask our backs to form a pocket by placing the inside arm up across his chest parallel to the ground and the outside arm down about waist high parallel to the ground. Thus, a pocket is formed in the stomach area and the quarterback is responsible for placing the ball in the pocket area. Once the ball is placed in the pocket, the ball should be grasped firmly by the ball carrier with both the top and bottom hands.

We tell our quarterbacks to give the ball to the runner; never let him take the ball from you. We want the quarterback to assume the responsibility of the handoff unless the ball carrier allows him to pass the ball through the pocket area and out the other side.

Now let's look at our quarterback's running offense. The quarterback has only three plays that he can call where he definitely carries the football. Counting the possibilities of the option keep, he has five plays in which he can possibly carry the ball. They are the 41 option, 49 option (diagrammed in Chapter 5), and the three that we will diagram shortly, 41 keeper, 47 keeper, and 25.

Play Call: Right or Left 41 Keeper (Diagrams 8-4 and 8-5)

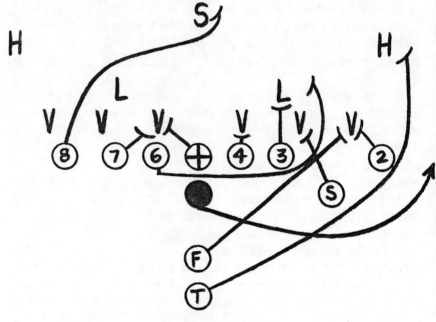

Diagram 8-4

Blocking Rules for 41 Keeper

   2 End—first man to inside

   3 Tackle—gap, over, outside

   4 Guard—gap, over, outside

   5 Center—over, back side

   6 Guard—pull and lead (block to the inside)

   7 Tackle—pull and seal for 6 guard

   8 End—safety or opposite halfback

   Slotback—protect gap, block man in slot area

   Fullback—first man past 2 end, no man past 2 end, double-team with 2
      end

   Tailback—block on corner if necessary, otherwise your halfback

   Quarterback—reverse pivot, keep the ball, and cut off blocks of fullback
      and tailback

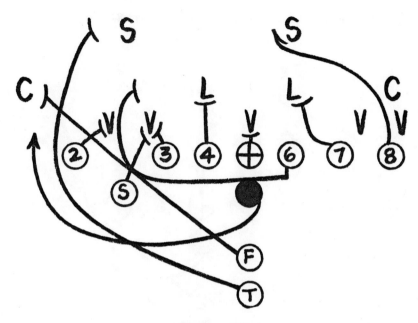

Diagram 8-5

Coaching Points: The line blocking rules are the same as a 41 so no new rules have to be taught for this play. The quarterback should sprint out and cut off the blocks of the fullback and the tailback. If defensive people are keying the tailback heavily, then have him cut to the inside to block, allowing the quarterback to run wide. We will sometimes confuse the defense that split second and get our quarterback free on the outside, especially if they are keying the fullback and tailback. This is not a play to be run more than a few times in a ball game. In fact, against certain teams you may not even want the play in your game plan. The scouting report and the opponent's defense may dictate whether or not you will use the play that particular week.

The next play, the 47 keeper, has been more successful than the 41 keeper because of the inside fake to the tailback which tends to pull the defensive people inside. This will allow the quarterback to fake to the tailback and keep the ball going to the outside.

Play Call: Right or Left 47 Keeper (Diagrams 8-6 and 8-7)

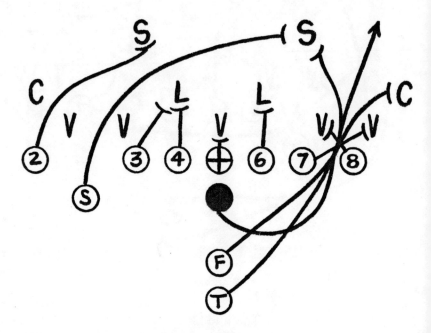

Diagram 8-6

Blocking Rules for 47 Keeper

    2 End—safety or opposite halfback

    3 Tackle—gap, over, linebacker

    4 Guard—gap, over, linebacker

    5 Center—strong-side gap, over, fill area

    6 Guard—gap, over, linebacker

    7 Tackle—cross-block with 8 end

    8 End—cross-block with 7 tackle

    Slotback—release downfield for safety or opposite halfback

    Fullback—fake a 47 blocking on the linebacker

    Tailback—fake a 47 blocking on linebacker if fullback needs help, otherwise block playside halfback

    Quarterback—fake a 47, keep the ball and cut upfield at the cross block

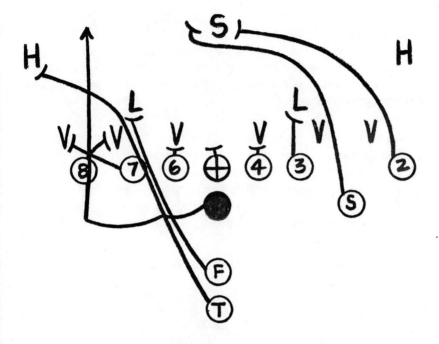

Diagram 8-7

Coaching Points: The 47 keep could be called a 28 but we have the linemen block the same as a 47 so to keep things simple for them we merely call it a 47 keep. The key to a good play is the fake of the 47 by the fullback and the tailback. If the 47 play has been a good gainer for the offense, then the defense will be keying on the fullback and the tailback very heavily. This will tend to draw the defense inside setting up a good cross block between the 7 tackle and the 8 end and allowing the quarterback to make a considerable gain on the play. On the cross-block technique, the 8 end always goes first and the 7 tackle actually pulls to the outside and blocks the defensive end. The quarterback should run through the cross block and then cut off the downfield blocking.

The common mistake by the quarterback is not setting up the 47 keeper properly. He should run the 47 several times making the defense aware of the inside play before the keeper will be

successful. However, on a few occasions we have run the 47
keeper several times and then come back inside with the 47. It
can be very confusing for the opponent's defense.

A split formation, red formation, can be run very successfully if the defense is rotating to the split or 2 end side. We like to
get this rotation and then run back away from the defensive
rotation.

The last running play that we give to the quarterbacks is a
quick-hitting trap play right up the middle of the defense. If
people overload their defenses on the outside, which many do,
we can run up the middle after faking a play to the outside. The
25 can be run from either a right or left formation and is especially effective from a spread formation, red, white, or blue.

Play Call: Right or Left 25 (Diagrams 8-8 and 8-9)

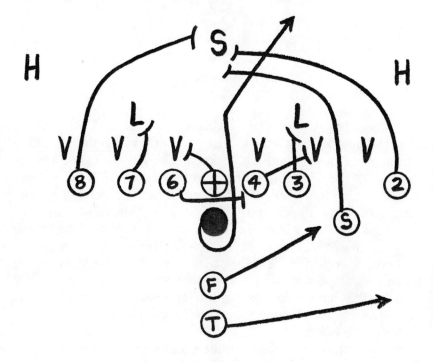

Diagram 8-8

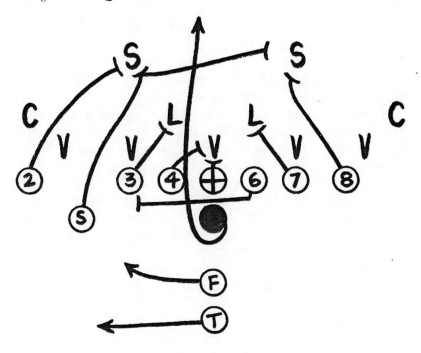

Diagram 8-9

Blocking Rules for 25

2 End—safety or your halfback

3 Tackle—linebacker inside

4 Guard—if man over, block man on or outside 3 tackle, no man over, drive block man on 5 center

5 Center—over, seal for 6 guard

6 Guard—pull and trap first lineman past 5 center

7 Tackle—linebacker inside

8 End—safety, your halfback

Slotback—safety, or opposite halfback

Fullback—fake a 41

Tailback—fake a 41

Quarterback—fake a 41 with a reverse pivot, complete pivot and run up the middle

Coaching Points: The key to this play is the quick trap block by the 6 guard and the faking action of the quarterback. The play is especially effective against some type of wide-tackle 6-2 defense where the middle is fairly open anyway. It can be run effectively against an odd-man or 5-man front if the blocking is performed properly and quickly. The quarterback must reverse pivot to get out of the way of the pulling 6 guard and may have to make a slight hesitation to allow the 6 guard to clear. We have found that if he makes a good pitch fake to the tailback, the play will be timed correctly. We have also made the quarterback pivot slightly deeper in order to time the play correctly.

This concludes our quarterback running offense except for the possible quarterback keep on the option plays. We do not like to have the quarterback running very much but do like to keep defenses off guard and let the quarterback run on occasion. If you are blessed with a large, strong quarterback then let him keep the ball and run more often.

9

Organizing and Executing
Special Slot I Plays

As you can see, our running game is not complicated or fancy. We believe in a sound running attack that is developed for safe ball handling to insure proper execution with a minimum number of errors. To accomplish this ball-control type of offensive attack, we strive for consistency of execution, and therefore, limit the running attack to the basic formations with a limited number of plays.

When the basic attack has been mastered, we then add a new play or two for use against our next opponent. In the past, we have had a tendency to overlook reverses and misdirection plays for our offensive running attack. However, we do add these types of plays once the basic running plays have been mastered.

We will show you, now, some of the special plays that we have run successfully during the past few years. Since adding the 41 option or triple option, we have developed an end-around reverse that comes off the triple option play. We especially like to run this with the triple option technique but it can be run equally effectively from the belly option technique. Again, remember that we do not teach both the triple option technique and the belly option technique. If our quarterback can handle the triple option technique, then we do not use the belly option technique. If he cannot handle the triple option, then we teach only the belly option. Therefore, we teach only the end-around from the option technique that we are using in the running attack.

We will show the end-around technique run both ways and

from both a right and left formation against both an odd - and even-front defense. In Diagrams 9-1 and 9-2 we will show it with the belly option technique and in Diagrams 9-3 and 9-4 from the triple option technique.

Play Call: Right or Left End-Around (Diagrams 9-1 through 9-4)

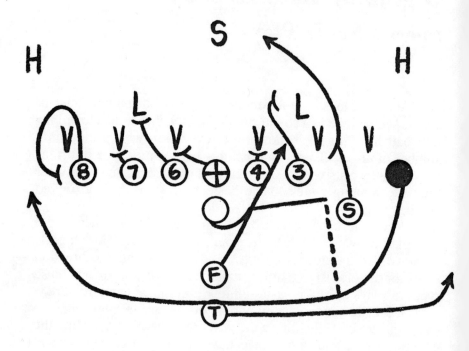

Diagram 9-1

Before giving the line and backfield blocking rules, notice that the only difference in the belly option end-around (Diagrams 9-1 and 9-2) and the triple option end-around (Diagrams 9-3 and 9-4) is the action of the quarterback. On the belly option technique, the quarterback is using the reverse pivot technique and on the triple option technique the quarterback is stepping at 45 de-

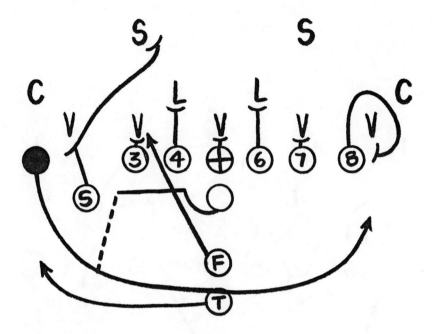

Diagram 9-2

grees toward the fullback then on out as in a 41 option. Remember, teach the end-around like the option that you are using, either the belly option or the triple option.

Blocking Rules for End-Around

   2 End—ball carrier, pull deep and take pitch from the quarterback, cut off 8 end's block

   3 Tackle—gap, over, outside

   4 Guard—gap, over, linebacker, outside

   5 Center—weak-side gap, over, fill area

   6 Guard—gap, over, linebacker, outside

   7 Tackle—gap, over, outside

   8 End—release around defensive end, then block back on him

   Slotback—brush block man in slot area, then release on safety or opposite halfback

Fullback—fake the 41 option
Tailback—fake the 41 option
Quarterback—fake the 41 option and pitch to the 2 end coming back
    around

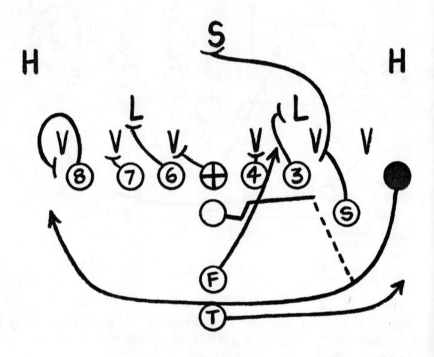

Diagram 9-3

Coaching Points: This is a very easy play to teach because it
is man-for-man blocking and the only new techniques to teach at
all are the 2 end and the 8 end. The 8 end merely releases
downfield, so that the defense will read option and begin their
rotation, then hooks back toward the sideline and blocks back in
on the defensive end. He should never go more than 3 to 5 yards
downfield before hooking back. The distance downfield is governed by the ends' speed and the speed of the play. If the 2 end

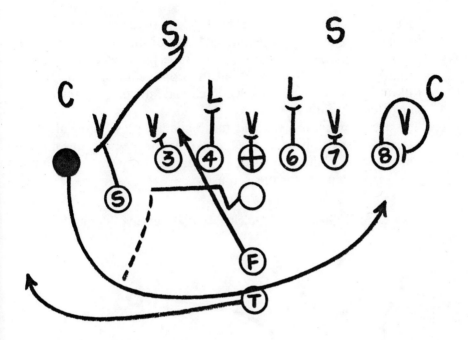

Diagram 9-4

comes deep enough, the 8 end's block will be very easy to execute. The defensive end will turn to the outside making the 8 end's block almost a screen block. The 8 end should be taught to put his head on the defensive end's numbers so that a penalty is not called.

The 2 end should pull deep on the snap count and come around looking for the pitch from the quarterback. His route should take him just inside the tailback and timing is very important. If the 2 end is very quick, he may have to delay at the line of scrimmage for a count or two before coming back.

The rest of the backfield,—fullback, tailback, quarterback, merely fake the option whether it be the belly or the triple option technique.

Another play that has been very good for us is a simple quick-pitch play. After the season is under way and people have scouted us a couple of times, we find many teams keying on our fullback with the back-side linebacker. This happens because our fullback is usually around the ball some place when the play is actually run. When we see that the opponent's linebackers are following the fullback, then we like to add the quick-pitch play to our offensive attack.

Remember that we add these special plays only after the basic offense has been learned, and that the special plays may be run only two or three times in a ball game. They are somewhat of a surprise element for our offense.

Play Call: Right or Left Quick Pitch (Diagrams 9-5 and 9-6)

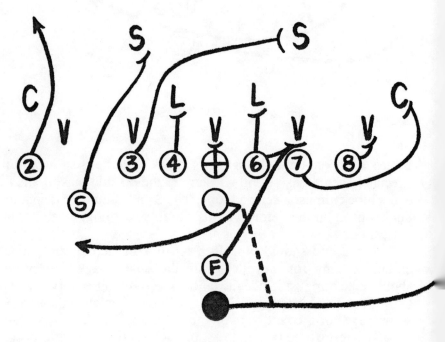

Diagram 9-5

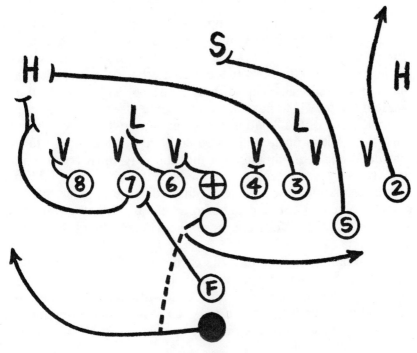

Diagram 9-6

Blocking Rules for Quick Pitch

2 End—release downfield at your halfback

3 Tackle—release inside for opposite halfback

4 Guard—gap, over, linebacker

5 Center—weak-side gap, over, reach block man on 6 Guard

6 Guard—linebacker

7 Tackle—pull and lead

8 End—reach block the defensive end

Slotback—release downfield for safety

Fullback—drive at 7 tackle and block anyone in that area

Tailback—take a quick pitch from the quarterback and cut off the blocks of 8 end and 7 tackle, run to daylight

Quarterback—step and make a hand fake at fullback then pitch and use bootleg action

Coaching Points: The importance of this particular play is that it must be executed with extreme quickness in order to be very effective. The fullback must really fire into the line in order to clear the quarterback so that the quarterback can make a quick pitch to the tailback. The tailback must be very close to the 7 tackle if the play is to have a certain degree of success. The reach or hook block of the 8 end is very important to this play. The end must tie the legs of the defensive end and not let him go to the outside. This is another reason that the play must be executed quickly,—the 8 end cannot hold the block for very long and if his defensive man releases inside off the block the tailback must be outside so he can not be caught from behind. The play should be so quick that the blocks are more like a screen block in basketball.

The tailback, once past the corner, should look toward the strong side for some downfield blocking. We have the slotback, the 3 tackle and the 2 end all coming downfield for blocking. We rely on this downfield blocking to get a long gainer. Even though the 3 tackle is not a speedy person, in most cases, he can still get some downfield blocking.

The fullback should always pick up anyone shooting through on the play side. In other words, he should actually try and seal off anyone on the play side from getting through to the tailback. The quarterback should use a bootleg action opposite the play after the pitch. On a very few occasions, we have let the quarterback bootleg off this play and either run or pass with the 2 end and slotback.

As one can readily see, there are many things that can be done offensively from the Slot I formation. We have found that we must be very careful because with the great number of things that can be done offensively one tends to clutter the running attack with too much junk. The junk or special plays are not really very valuable if the basic offensive attack is not executed properly.

The last thing that we would like to include in this chapter is our draw play from our passing attack. It is not really a special play in the sense of the quick pitch and the end-around because it is a part of our basic running attack. We will put it in this section and then will have all the running plays that are a part of our offensive attack. We do run a sprint-out and play-action passing attack as you will see in Chapters 10 and 11 so our draw is developed off the 41 play.

Play Call: Right or Left 41 Draw (Diagrams 9-7 and 9-8)

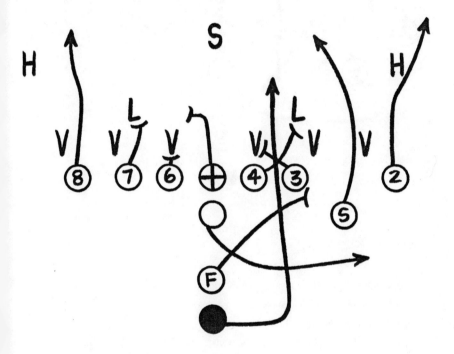

Diagram 9-7

Blocking Rules for 41 Draw

    2 End—release downfield on a flag pattern, responsible for your half-back

    3 Tackle—cross-block with 4 guard, block man over 4

    4 Guard—cross-block with 3 tackle, block linebacker over 3

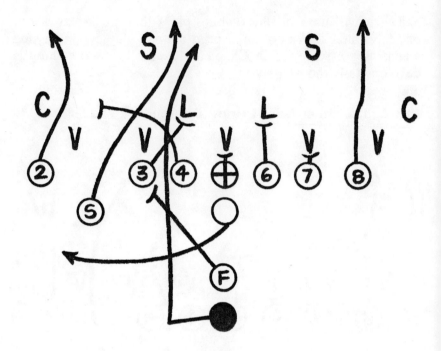

Diagram 9-8

5 Center—over, weak-side linebacker

6 Guard—over, fill area

7 Tackle—over, linebacker, fill area

8 End—release on streak pattern, responsible for your halfback

Slotback—release down the middle, responsible for safety

Fullback—block first man outside three tackle

Tailback—take three steps toward sideline, square to line of scrimmage, take handoff and run to daylight

Quarterback—take three steps, square to sideline, hand to tailback, continue out

Coaching Points: The important thing in this play is the quarterback-tailback exchange. We teach our tailback to take three steps toward the sideline then turn toward the line of scrimmage so that his shoulders are parallel to the line of scrimmage. He should let the quarterback place the ball in the pocket formed by his arms and then cut to the hole in the 4 guard-3 tackle area. The tailback must be shown where the hole most likely will be against the defenses that your opponent is playing, to give him some idea where to cut.

The quarterback reverse pivots and takes three steps toward the tailback then turns so his shoulders are parallel to the sideline before handing to the tailback. He is responsible for putting the ball in the tailback's pocket and then should continue out toward the sideline. You may have to adjust the steps of your quarterbacks and tailbacks to get the correct handoff position. We always strive for the 3-3 step but have had to make ajustments for certain tailbacks and quarterbacks.

The ends and slotback are given quite a lot of freedom as far as a route and technique are concerned. They know that they must block or use some other method to take care of the defensive halfbacks and safety. We allow them to run the defenders deep if they will follow, and in high school competition, we have found that the defenders will often follow the three people almost out of the ball park.

The lineblocking is also very important in this particular draw play. The 3 tackle and the 4 guard are taught a cross-block technique. On the cross-block technique, the 3 tackle always will go in front of the 4 guard. The tackle will block down on the man over the 4 guard. On a six-man front this will be a down lineman and on a five-man front this will be a linebacker. We have found that this is a very effective way for the 3 tackle to block. The 4 guard will go behind the 3 tackle and block the man in the 3-tackle area. On a six-man front, the 4 guard will block the inside linebacker and on a five-man front he more often than not will block the corner linebacker, as in Diagram 9-8. The remainder of the line is one-on-one blocking with the 6 guard and 7 tackle showing pass blocking with a drop step then block.

The fullback must block the man outside or on the 3 tackle. He must be shown that on a five-man front his block will be the lineman in the 3-tackle area who may be head-up on the 3 tackle.

With the cross block and the fullback kicking the defensive

man out there is quite a hole for the tailback to run for. Once through the line, the tailback is free to cut to either sideline or to run down the middle if it is open.

One final point before leaving the special plays, and we cannot stress this enough; don't clutter the offense with a lot of special, or fancy plays just to have a number or variety of plays. Add a special play only if it will have special benefit against this week's opponent; otherwise go with the basic running offense.

10

Running Basic Pass Patterns
from the Slot I Offense

Up to this point, the Slot I offense has been considered only as a running offense. The Slot I formation does, however, have great potential as a passing offense. We feel that the three quick receivers: the 2 end, the 8 end, and the slotback give the formation unlimited passing potential. With the use of more complex and stunting defenses, it has become increasingly more important that any successful running offense be complemented by a well organized and consistent passing attack. It used to be that a good running game could carry a team to victory almost any day, but today, a running attack cannot be expected to punch out gain after gain unless the defense is spread and continuously threatened by the use of a good passing attack. The ever improving defenses have made it more and more important to develop a strong passing attack to complement the running attack, even at the high school level.

The passing attack described in this and the next chapter was not designed as an elaborate passing offense, but rather as a complement to our strong Slot I running game.

There are three basic ways to pass the football; by drop-back action, sprint-out action, and by the play-action pass. For many years we used only the play-action passing technique and, if you are only going to use one technique for your passing game, then we would strongly recommend the play-action passing technique. We will present our play-action passing game in Chapter 11 for those of you who are interested only in the play-action passing game.

This past year we had a quarterback who was an above average runner so we implemented the sprint-out action passing game in our offensive attack. Not wanting to give up our play-action passing game because it had been so good to us, we now have both a sprint-out passing game and a play-action passing attack. If the sprint out continues to be as successful the next year or two, we will probably drop the play-action attack and keep only the sprint-out passing technique in our offense attack.

In this chapter, we are going to cover the sprint-out passing attack that we are currently using with the Slot I running game. There are several advantages to the sprint-out attack:

1. The offense is running away from one-half the blocking problems. By using the sprint-out technique, the quarterback is running away from the back-side rush thus eliminating one-half of the defensive pass rush. If we are eliminating one-half of the pass rush, then we feel that we are also eliminating one-half of our pass-blocking problems. This in turn makes the teaching of the pass-blocking techniques only one-half as tough a job.

2. We spend less practice time developing the sprint-out attack than would have to be spent on a drop-back passing attack. We spend less time protecting the passer because he is running away from one-half of the pass rush. Also, the blockers know the area that they must protect and we do not have to work against individual defensive stunts as long.

3. We always get the line of scrimmage back if the ball is not thrown. With the fullback and the tailback lead blocking, we have found that we can always get back to the original line of scrimmage even if the ball is not thrown. The defense is not making the big play and catching our passer for a loss.

4. It dictates what the defense must do to stop your attack. The sprint series puts great pressure on the defensive perimeters—corners, halfbacks, ends, and outside linebackers—because they are responsible for both the run and the pass. If they are going to stop the sprint-out passing attack, then they must put more people on the corners. Therefore, we are dictating the type of defense that they must play against us. Once they overload the perimeters, then our inside running game will be very strong.

5. Less quarterback skill is required. Because the ball will travel about one-half the distance of a drop-back pass, our quarterbacks need not have as much passing skill to complete the pass. We actually teach the basic sprint action to our quarterbacks as a run, first, and a pass, second.

6. It capitalizes on a good running quarterback. With the quarterback as a run threat, there is more run threat than the drop-back passing attack has. The drop-back attack has only one threat and that is the draw play. The sprint-out attack has at least two, and possibly three or four, run threats. The quarterback is always a run threat, the tailback is a draw threat, the fullback could be a draw threat, and finally, the slotback could be brought back for a reverse or counter threat.

Keep in mind that the above mentioned advantages are not necessarily in the order of importance.

Before getting into the sprint-out pass patterns, let's consider the three basic ingredients of a successful passing attack. The passing attack must have (1) a passer; (2) a receiver or receivers; and (3) pass protection for the passer. Now let's look at these three basic ingredients individually.

THE PASSER

If you are fortunate enough to have a quarterback who is an above average passer, then the ideas and techniques to be discussed in this section need not necessarily apply. However, what we are covering in this section are suggestions for developing the quarterback with below average ability into a respectable passer. The good passer should be conscientious about three things; how to grip the ball; how to throw the ball; and the proper footwork for throwing the ball.

The Grip

When gripping the football, the quarterback should always have the last two fingers on the laces of the ball. The index finger should be approximately one inch from the end of the football. There should be a spread between the index finger and the second finger. The index finger should be the last finger to leave the ball as the quarterback releases his pass. This index finger controls the course and direction of the ball. The index finger, along with the thumb, should construct a 90-degree angle if the quarterback has the proper grip on the ball. The ball should be gripped on the top one-fourth and the quarterback should have a soft squeeze on the ball—not a death grip as is common with some quarterbacks. The ball is held in the fingers and not in the palm of the hand. The quarterback should always use the same grip regardless of whether he is throwing a long, medium, or a short pass.

The Throwing Motion

As our quarterback receives the center snap, we want him to bring the ball right up to his numbers with the ball in both hands. As he gets ready to release the football, he will bring the ball up from the numbers to the area near the ear. He is taught not to get the ball too close to the ear and not to cramp the arm by having the ball too close to the ear. The nose of the ball should be slightly up. As the ball is released, the wrist should turn out slightly putting the proper spin on the football. The ball should be near the top of the helmet and should be released slightly ahead of the helmet. This release is the only phase the passer should change for a long, medium or short pass. The angle of the arm at the release determines a long, medium, or a short pass. The arm release for a short pass is quick and the ball is approximately parallel to the ground or 90 degrees. The long pass is thrown on an angle of approximately 130 degrees which will keep the nose of the ball up on the release. The medium pass should be released about halfway between the long and the short pass, or at approximately 110 degrees.

The Footwork

Probably the most important item in developing a respectable passer is the correct footwork. For our sprint-out series, we want the quarterback to get away from the center quickly. Because he will sprint out both right and left, we want the quarterback in a parallel stance, with his weight on the balls of the feet. We do not care how the quarterback clears the center. We have had some quarterbacks who used a false step forward then a pivot and move out to the release point and we have had some who merely pivoted and sprinted out to the release point. As long as the quarterback clears the center, we allow for individual differences.

The quarterback should always sprint out to the area from which the ball will be thrown and then set up to pass. This release area is slightly outside the 3 tackle in the area vacated by the slotback running the pass pattern. At the release area, the feet should be shoulder-width apart. The quarterback should be on balance with the weight on the back foot. As the ball is released, the quarterback should step toward his receiver or target with the front foot and push off the back foot. A right-handed passer then should step toward the receiver with the left foot, pushing off his right foot as the ball is released. A common fault of many quarterbacks is to overstride with the left foot and it is much better to understride than to overstride. Therefore, we check our quarterbacks and see that they are taking a short stride rather than a long stride.

If we are using a play-action pass instead of the sprint-out pass, the footwork is different up to the release point because the quarterback must make a play fake to either the fullback, or tailback, or both. Once the quarterback has made the proper play fake, the footwork remains the same.

Regardless of how good your quarterback may be as a passer, you should constantly check and correct his fundamental passing techniques. The following items are most important and should be constantly checked by the backfield or quarterback coach:

1. Does the passer get to the release area as soon as possible?
2. Does he have the ball ready to pass immediately?
3. Does he grip the ball properly?
4. Does the ball rotate properly—with proper wrist action?
5. Does he keep his feet close together and step correctly at the release?
6. Does he keep the ball in both hands as long as possible to avoid the fumble?
7. Does he throw on balance and follow through correctly?
8. Does he locate the open receiver and deliver the ball as soon as the receiver is open?

9. Does he know what to do if no receiver is open; (a) run;
   (b) throw the ball away; (c) eat the ball; etc.?
10. Does he release the ball correctly for the long, medium,
    and short passes?

We feel that if the time is spent showing the quarterback the proper grip, release, and footwork along with the proper mental preparation of when to throw and when not to throw the football, any quarterback can become an adequate passer.

THE PASS RECEIVER

It has been said often that a team's passing attack is only as good as the passer. However, we feel that that statement should also be expanded to include the pass receivers. Without good pass receivers, the above average passer is of little or no value to the team because there is no one to catch the football. On the other hand, a great pass receiver can make a below average passer into a respectable passer.

When selecting pass receivers, 2 end, 8 end, and slotback in our offense, there are two characteristics that we look for: (1) can he catch the football? (2) does he have above average speed? The first of these, catching the ball, of course, is the more important of the two. Great pass receivers seem to have an abundance of natural ability. We have found, however, that through hard work and patience anyone can become an adequate pass receiver. Probably the most important point for a pass receiver to re-member, is always to look the ball into his hands. The receiver should always be taught to catch the ball with the fingers and not to trap the ball against the chest or pads. As we often say, be sure you catch the ball, then run. Many young receivers will take their eyes off the ball too soon because they are looking for a place to run.

We also consider speed as a quality of a good receiver. Maybe the word speed is somewhat misleading. We look for quickness. Before any receiver can catch the football, he must be able to release from the line of scrimmage and run a good pass pattern. Again, the great receivers seem to have the native ability to get this done but, through hard work, any pass receiver can develop the ability to release and run a good pass route. If the defense is attempting to jam the receivers and keep them from leaving the line of scrimmage, there are two ways to attack the problem. Probably the simplest method is to split the receiver away from the main body of the defense. We very seldom have defensive people attempt to jam our 2 end because of his split. The slotback and the 8 end are often jammed on the line of scrimmage however. We can split our 8 end by using a blue or white formation but our slotback is never split. Therefore, the other method that we use to get off the line of scrimmage is to use one or more faking maneuvers. There are numerous fakes that can be taught but we use what are probably the three most common ones;

1. Head and Shoulder Fake—This is the easiest method to use and to teach as far as we are concerned. After the snap, the receiver makes a quick movement of his head and shoulders in the direction opposite of which he wishes to go. If he wants to release to the outside or right, then he makes the head and shoulder fake to the left, then quickly steps to the outside or right around the defensive man. We also like our receiver to use this fake on the defensive halfbacks downfield to get open on his pass route.

2. Pull Technique—This technique is also very simple for the receiver to learn. On the snap of the ball, he merely pulls to the outside around the defensive man. This technique is the same as our pulling linemen use. If our receiver is pulling to the right, he takes a short step right with the right foot, pivots, and moves out to the right until he clears the defensive man. If this is done quickly, it will usually free the pass receiver.

3. Spin Out—After the snap, our receiver completes a 360-degree turn and drives to the inside or outside of the defensive man. If the spin is done quickly it is almost impossible for the defensive man to jam the receiver on the line of scrimmage.

We have also, on rare occasions, sent our slotback in motion so that the defense cannot jam him on the line of scrimmage.

The slotback has the most trouble of our receivers releasing from the line. The defense knows that he is one of the primary receivers most of the time and quite often tries to jam him on the line. Again, hard work will get the slotback and ends some techniques for releasing from the line of scrimmage.

After clearing the line of scrimmage, the next step is to run the correct route. The young receivers have a great tendency to run their pass routes in a lazy fashion, making roundhouse cuts and slowing down after their cuts are made. To help correct these faults, we use cones and chalk lines and have our receivers run the lines and make the proper cuts. Again, nothing can substitute for hard work and proper coaching.

The last thing we spend a great amount of time on is putting the ball safely away after it has been caught. If the ball is being put under the right arm, we want our receiver to cover the front point of the ball with his right hand. He then applies pressure on the ball with the right elbow and holds the ball against his right side. We do not want the ball swung around like a loaf of bread. Keep it in close to the body and, if possible, cover it with the left hand and body before being hit or tackled.

We can probably best summarize the pass-receiving technique by giving the tips that we give to all our pass receivers in their play books.

Tips for the Pass Receivers

1. Whether you become a good receiver depends directly upon the amount of extra work you do.
2. The most important point to remember is to look the ball into your hands.
3. Practice tucking the ball away and explode for extra yardage.
4. Work on catching the badly thrown pass, make a spectacular catch become routine.
5. Work to improve your weaknesses.
6. Know the depth of the route you are to run.
7. When the passer is trapped, come back to help him, find an open spot with a clear line of sight.
8. Peel back, block for the receiver shorter than you or for the quarterback run.
9. Learn to relax the fingers and hands while receiving the ball.

10. Learn to run under control and break at top speed.

11. Do not slow yourself down by running with arms extended, reach for the ball on the last step.

12. Release from the line of scrimmage low, explode, you must not be held up or jammed, drop one shoulder to make yourself small.

13. When challenged for the ball, be aggressive, it is yours. If you cannot catch it, do not allow the opponents to catch it either.

14. If the ball is not thrown to you, be a blocker.

15. Develop the attitude that you can catch anything you can touch.

16. Catch the ball at its highest point.

17. Look for the ball immediately on a pass cut.

PASS PROTECTION

The pass protection for our sprint-out series and play-action passes comes from the five interior linemen plus the fullback and the tailback. This gives us seven people to block for our quarterback. First, let's consider the blocking for our sprint-out passing series. Since our sprint series is taught as a run-pass series, the play-side linemen, the 3 tackle, 4 guard, and the 5 center, block as they would on a running play. They should fire out on the snap count and aggressively block their assignments on the line of scrimmage. If the lineman's responsibility is a linebacker, he should fire out as if to block the linebacker and then hold up and fill his area. Because of the pass possibility the lineman cannot go downfield after the linebacker. The back-side linemen, the 6 guard and the 7 tackle, are taught to area block. The area-block technique is similar to the block used to protect a drop-back passer. We teach our linemen to drop-step away from the line of scrimmage and protect their inside gaps. If no one comes to the inside gap, they pick up the first man to their outside. With this type of block, we want the knees bent, head up, hips low, and the shoulders square to the line of scrimmage. The feet should be moving with short, choppy steps to maintain proper balance. As the defensive player comes, we want our people to butt him on the numbers, then retreat slightly and butt him on the numbers again, etc. We have our 5 center pull and protect to the back side

if no one is in his area. By doing this, the center can cut down the
back-side rush that possibly could catch the quarterback from the
blind side. On all pass plays our line blocking rules are:

> 3 Tackle—gap, over, fill area
>
> 4 Guard—gap, over, fill area
>
> 5 Center—over, pull to back side
>
> 6 Guard—gap, over, fill area
>
> 7 Tackle—gap, over, fill area.

On the sprint-out series, we have our fullback fill and block
directly outside the hip of the 3 tackle. The tailback will then fill
at the outside hip of the fullback and block anyone in that area. If
no one shows up for either or both of the backs to block, they
should continue on downfield and the quarterback should follow
with the run.

We want our pass blockers to occupy their defensive men
for five seconds before releasing them. They should try to tie up
their feet if at all possible so that they cannot get in the pursuit
lanes. Once the quarterback throws the football, he yells
"BALL" and all linemen pursue, looking for the possible downfield block and to stop the return of the possible interception. The
quarterback and the tailback are responsible for the sideline in
case of the interception.

On our play-action passes (Chapter 11), the line blocking
rules remain the same. The only difference is the action of the
fullback, tailback, and the quarterback. With a play-action pass,
the backs must carry out the play fake before the quarterback can
set up to pass.

CALLING THE PASS PLAY

Our quarterback calls the pass play by using a three-digit
number. Our patterns are numbered 100, 200, 300, etc. So the
quarterback, in the huddle, would give the information, either
right or left, then the pass pattern that he wants run. A sample
call for a sprint out pass might be: RIGHT, 100, ON 2. This
would tell the offense that the basic formation was right, the

receivers to run the 100 pattern, and the snap count is on 2. If the quarterback wants to split both ends he would make this call: RIGHT, BLUE, 100, on 1. This BLUE call would tell the two ends to split.

If the quarterback wants to call a play-action pass, he would add the backfield action that he desires like this: RIGHT, 133, on 2. This tells the offense the basic formation was right, the ends and slotback to run a 100 pattern, the fullback and tailback to fake a 33, and the snap count is 2. We have found that this is a very simple method of calling both the sprint-out and the play-action passes.

In this chapter, we are going to give the basic sprint-out series. The eight people who are not receivers do exactly the same thing on every sprint-out pass call. We will diagram their responsibilities from both a right and a left formation to show the areas that they are responsible for.

Before we diagram our pass patterns, remember that we also flip-flop our passing offense. We can run any pattern to either the right or left side. So with this in mind, we will diagram each pattern from a right and a left formation. Remember also that we can split either or both ends and run the same pattern by merely adding the words, RED, WHITE, or BLUE, to the quarterback's call in the huddle.

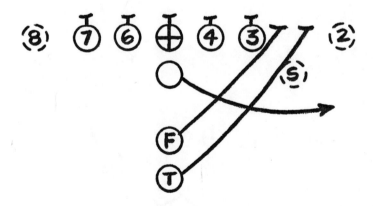

Diagram 10-1: Right Formation

Diagram 10-2: Left Formation

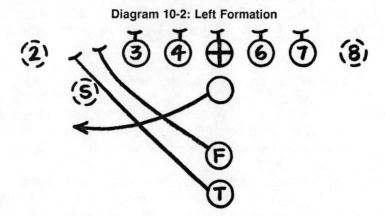

Play Call: Right or Left 100 (Diagrams 10-3 and 10-4)

Coaching Points: This is a very good pattern against a three-deep secondary. The 2 end going deep forces the halfback to stay back until the safety rotates over, thus allowing us to hit the slotback in the flat on a 5-yard pattern. If the halfback comes

Diagram 10-3

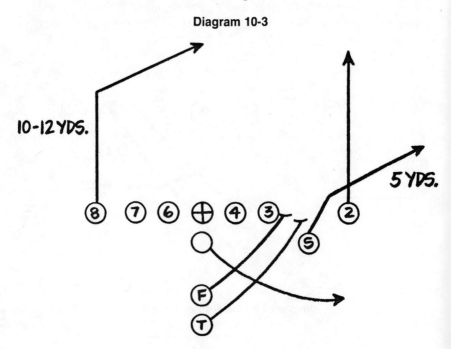

Diagram 10-4

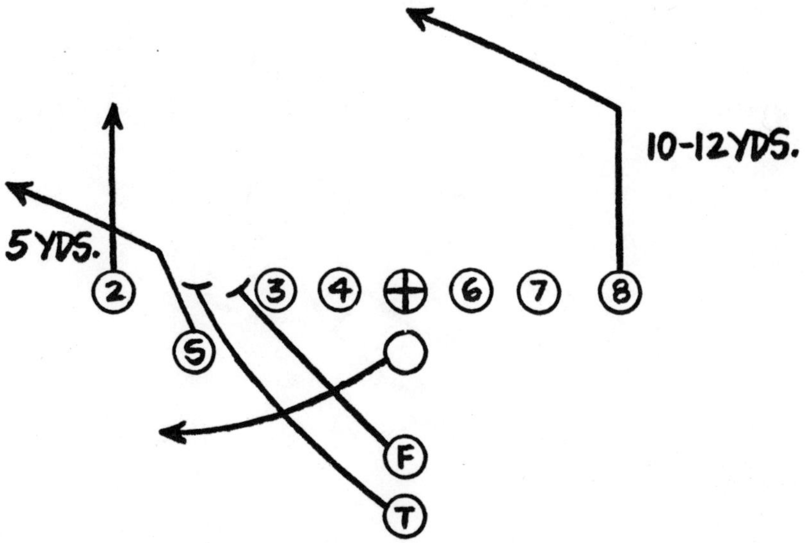

10-12YDS.

5YDS.

② ③ ④ ⊕ ⑥ ⑦ ⑧

Ⓢ

Ⓕ

Ⓣ

up immediately, then the 2 end should be open on the deep streak pattern. Also many times we have hit the 8 end coming across in the middle. The slotback should go about 3 yards and then cut for the sideline going no deeper than 5 to 6 yards. Anytime the ball is thrown to the slotback, the 2 and 8 ends should peel back and block. If the quarterback elects to run with the ball, the slotback, and the 2 and 8 ends should peel back looking for blocks.

Play Call: Right or Left 200 (Diagrams 10-5 and 10-6)

Coaching Points: We like the 200 pattern because it puts pressure on the defensive halfback on the slot side. The slotback and the 2 end cut at about the same time making the defensive halfback cover one of the two receivers. If the three-deep secondary is rotating toward the slot side, the 8 end coming through the middle is often wide open. Against a two-deep, corner defense the slotback is usually wide open. With our strong Slot I running game, most teams are playing either a two-deep, or a

Diagram 10-5

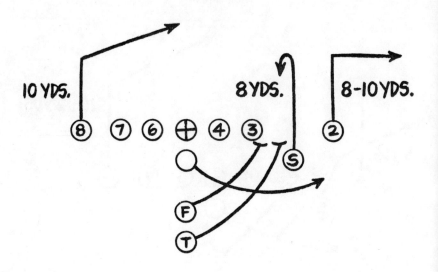

Diagram 10-6

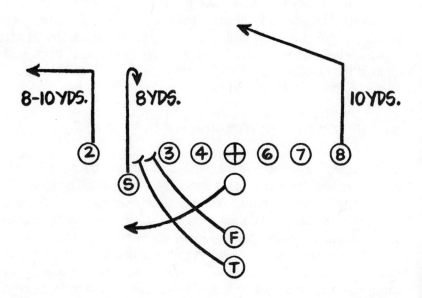

three-deep defense and eight- or nine-man fronts to contain the running game. We very seldom face a seven-man front with a four-deep secondary because it cannot contain our running game successfully.

Play Call: Right or Left 300 (Diagrams 10-7 and 10-8)

Coaching Points: On the 300 pattern, the slotback must hook to the outside and not allow himself to drift into the middle. The 2 end goes down 10 to 12 yards and then cuts toward the middle making the safety stay at home. The 8 end comes into the middle about 8 yards deep and should be wide open. If the defense is a 2 deep secondary, the slotback is often open because the defensive halfback has been told not to let anyone deeper than he is so he will go deep with the 2 end. We allow the slotback to drift toward the sideline if he does not get the ball on the hook.

Diagram 10-7

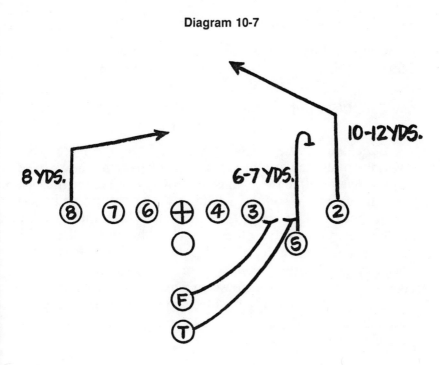

Diagram 10-8

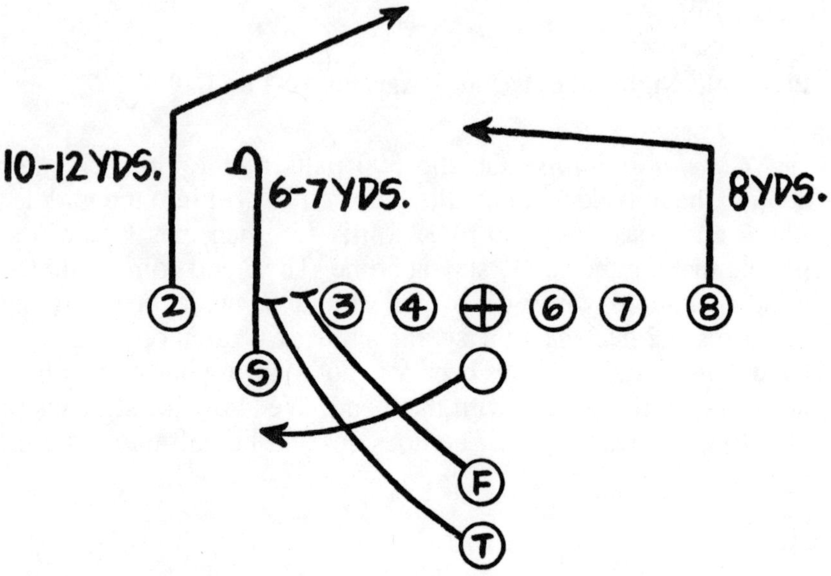

We want our 2 end and 8 end to use a head-and-shoulder fake before they make their cuts to help get them open.

Play Call: Right or Left 400 (Diagrams 10-9 and 10-10)

Coaching Points: The 400 pattern has given us more touchdowns the past three or four years than any pattern that we have. It is especially effective against the two-deep secondaries because the defensive halfbacks tend to go with our 2 and 8 end leaving the slotback open down the middle. Many times, we find the defense trying to cover the slotback with a linebacker and in that case the slotback definitely has the advantage. It is not an especially good pattern against a three-deep secondary but we have completed the sideline pass on a number of occasions. This is a very good pattern to use the blue and white formations on and spread the defenses even farther by splitting the 8 end and even the 2 end wider.

Diagram 10-9

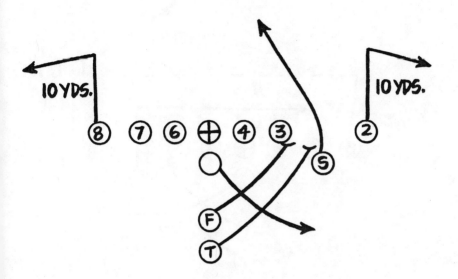

Diagram 10-10

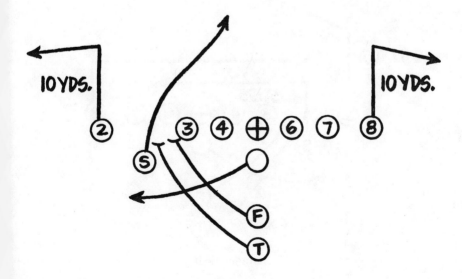

Play Call: Right or Left 800 (Diagrams 10-11 and 10-12)

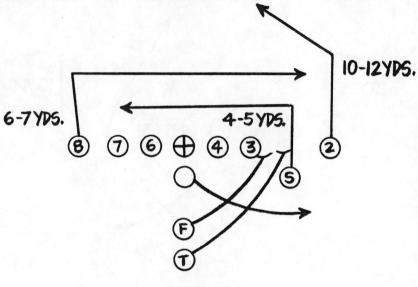

Diagram 10-11

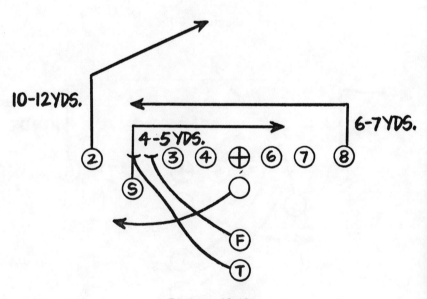

Diagram 10-12

Coaching Points: This pattern has been a very good pattern for a short gain (8 to 12 yards). The 2 end going deep and through the middle tends to make the halfback and the safety stay at home and not come up too fast. The crossing action of the slotback and the 8 end usually opens the 8 end in the vicinity of the 3 tackle or out toward the sideline. It is not the long gainer that the 400 pattern is but it can be used to keep the defensive people honest on first or second downs. If the defensive secondary comes up too fast, then the 2 end will be open deep and the result can be a touchdown.

Play Call: Right or Left 900 (Diagrams 10-13 and 10-14)

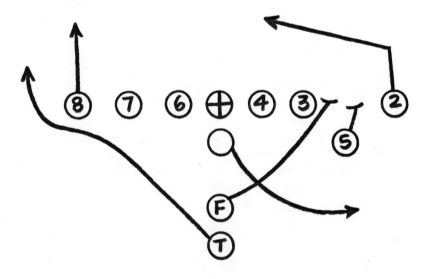

Diagram 10-13

Coaching Points: We added this pattern because we found that many defensive teams were keying the slotback to determine run or pass. If he blocked, the secondaries came up very quickly and if he released, they stayed at home expecting the pass. The pattern also gives our passing attack a throwback pass that tends

Diagram 10-14

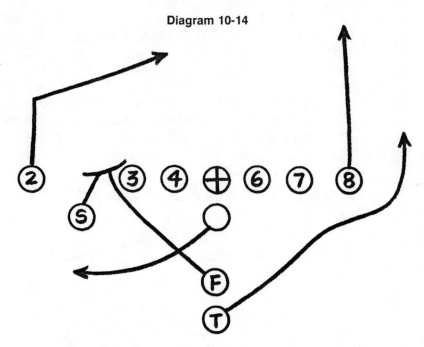

to keep the defensive secondaries at home a few seconds longer. The slotback will block in the area normally blocked by the tailback and the fullback will fill to the inside of the slotback. We will on occasion have the slotback block down and the fullback fill outside the slotback. The 2 end going down the middle tends to clear that area and the 8 end going straight down tends to take the defensive halfback deep. This is a very dangerous pass to throw because if it is intercepted then you have more than likely given up 6 points. The quarterback must not throw the ball unless he is positive that it cannot be intercepted. The pattern is not one that you should use several times a game. It also works very well from a blue or a white formation in which the 8 end is split.

This concludes our sprint-out passing attack. As you have seen, it is a very simple attack and it does complement our Slot I running attack. We do not pass just for the sake of passing but rather to help make our running game better by keeping the defense honest. It is a safe passing attack because most of the passes are only 8 to 10 yards in depth when the ball is thrown.

11

Running Play-Action Passes
in the Slot I

As was mentioned in the previous chapter, our play-action pass was our complete passing attack until we added the sprint-out series. Even though we strongly believe in keeping things simple, the play-action passing attack, along with the sprint-out passing attack, does not complicate our offensive passing attack. As you will see later in this chapter, we use the same pass patterns, with a couple of exceptions, that we use in our sprint-out series. We do this so that our receivers have to learn only one set of pass patterns. The only difference between our sprint-out passing attack and our play-action passing attack is the backfield and quarterback action.

Before giving you our play-action passing attack, we would like to give you some background information on it. When we were first trying to develop a passing attack, we wanted two things; simplicity and consistency. Since the backfield action had already been learned and since only one set of blocking rules had to be taught to the offensive linemen for the entire play-action passing attack, we had simplicity. By using several simple patterns and combining them with our play fakes, we do not have to spend a lot of practice time on our passing attack. This simplicity then allows us to spend more practice time on other aspects of the offense.

What really sold us on the play-action technique was the consistency that it gives to our offense. It is a natural complement to our Slot I running attack and it is an excellent short-yardage and goal-line passing attack. The play-action passing attack allows us to maintain possession, develop sustained drives, and consistently score from our side of the field. It allows us to keep the defense honest because the linebackers must think about covering the run possibility before they can release to their pass coverage points. A properly executed play-action pass will tend to freeze the linebackers or eliminate them completely from the pass coverage, allowing us to free receivers in the area between the linebackers and the secondary. Thus, on most occasions, our passes travel only a few yards which, in turn, adds consistency to the passing attack. It is much easier to complete the short pass than to throw and complete the deep pass.

The play-action pass also keeps the defense off balance. Because we can throw the ball off a play fake, we can also throw the ball on any down which keeps the defense guessing and off balance. We will throw on first or second down as well as on the third down and long-yardage situation. We will try to eliminate this third-and-long situation by throwing on earlier downs. When you have a strong running attack and will throw on any down, you will definitely keep the defense off balance.

We feel that there are three important factors essential to a play-action passing attack. First, the offense must have a strong running attack. If the defense is going to respect the play fake on the action pass, then the offensive running game must be a strong one and well executed. We feel that our Slot I running game is very strong and that the play action passing attack complements it very well.

Secondly, the faking of the backfield is very important. It is important for the backfield action to be exactly the same as in the companion running play. We stress faking as naturally as possible, both by the quarterback and the running backs—fullback and tailback. We would like our quarterbacks to keep the ball hidden from the defense as much as possible. We feel that this, combined with the faking of the other two backs, will convince the defenders that the play is a running play. This, in turn, will allow us to find an open receiver somewhere in the pattern.

Finally, the play of the offensive linemen is very important. It does little good to fake a running play with the backfield if the linemen are going to show pass too early. We try to avoid this by having our onside linemen fire out and aggressively block the defensive personnel. Of course, they must be told that they cannot go downfield to block on a pass. We allow our back-side guard and tackle to be somewhat less aggressive in their blocking but we would like them to show pass at the last possible moment.

CALLING THE PLAY-ACTION PASS

In calling the play-action pass, the quarterback merely adds the play fake desired to the pass pattern that he wants the receivers to run. As an example, if he wants the receivers to run a 100 pattern and the backfield to fake a 33, he will call for the pass play 133. The entire call by the quarterback in the huddle might go like this: RIGHT, BLUE, 133, ON 2. This would tell the offense that the basic formation is RIGHT; BLUE would tell the 2 and 8 ends to split from 10-12 yards; 133 would tell the receivers to run a 100 pattern and the backs to fake a 33; the snap count would be on 2.

One more sample call might go like this: LEFT, WHITE, 233, on 1. This call would tell the offense that the basic formation is LEFT: WHITE would tell the 8 end to split 10-12 yards; 233 would tell the receivers to run a 200 pattern and the backs to fake a 33; the snap count would be on 1.

By comparison, the sprint-out pass would be called a RIGHT, RED, 100, on 2 and the play action pass would be called a RIGHT, RED, 133, on 2. We have found that this is a very simple way to distinguish between the sprint-out and the play-action pass.

As you have probably already figured out, this method of calling play-action passes gives us almost an unlimited passing attack. We have six basic pass patterns and if we combine them with our fullback and tailback running plays, which number 13, we could have 78 possible pass plays. On any given day, we could run all 78 if we had to because we know the 13 running plays and we know the six basic pass patterns. What we generally do however, is to examine our opponent's defenses and use only those patterns that will be effective against the defenses that our opponent uses. Against this week's opponent, we may have only six or seven pass plays that will be effective. Our quarterback will know which plays will be most effective and will use those unless instructed to do otherwise.

CHAPTER FORMAT

What we will do in this chapter is to take a few of the most used pass plays and diagram them from a right and a left formation showing the basic pattern and the backfield action. Remember, our linemen's, blocking rules on all pass plays are:

3 Tackle—gap, over, fill area

4 Guard—gap, over, fill area

5 Center—over, pull and protect back side

6 Guard—gap, over, fill area

7 Tackle—gap, over, fill area

After some of the basic pass plays are diagrammed, we will also diagram our screen passes and our special pass plays.

Play Call: Right or Left 133 (Diagrams 11-1 and 11-2)

Coaching Points: The quarterback technique on our play-action passes is very simple. He will use the same action that the running play would use to about the inside hip of the 3 tackle and then fish-hook back to a depth of about 4 to 5 yards and set up to throw. This depth is governed somewhat by the speed and quickness of the quarterback, and each quarterback may set up a little differently as far as depth is concerned. The size of the quarterback also dictates the depth needed. A small quarterback would have to set up much deeper then a tall one simply because he could not see over the offensive and defensive personnel on the line of scrimmage.

Diagram 11-1

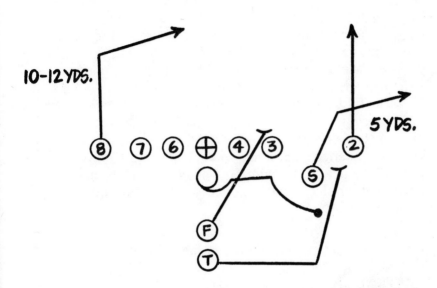

Diagram 11-2

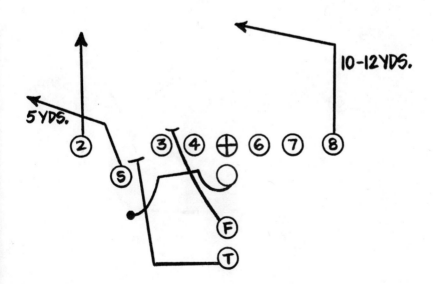

The tailback should run a correct route then break up toward the line of scrimmage and block ahead of the quarterback. This is also a rather simple technique to teach and only requires timing to provide adequate protection. The tailback will usually encounter the opponent's defensive end. He should try to turn the end to the outside and make him bring his arms down if at all possible. We are not too particular about the technique used as long as the tailback is getting the job done.

The fullback, after a good play fake, should help to seal the line of scrimmage in the area of the play fake. He can often block on a linebacker who has gone with the play fake.

The quarterback should always be taught to yell "Ball" once the ball is in the air. This allows the linemen to release downfield for blocks and to protect against the return of an intercepted pass.

Play Call: Right or Left 141 (Diagrams 11-3 and 11-4)

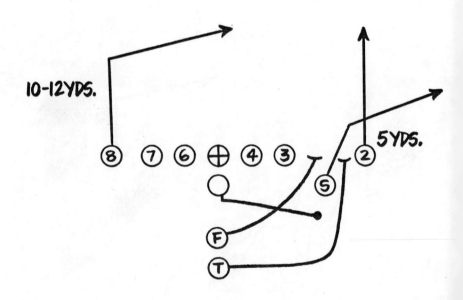

Diagram 11-3

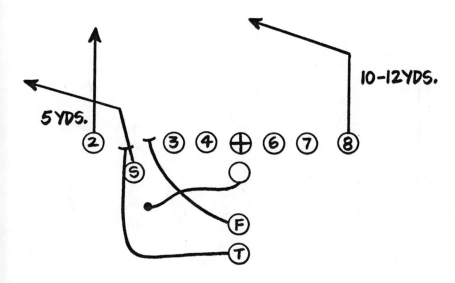

Diagram 11-4

Coaching Points: This particular pass play is very similar to the basic sprint-out pass pattern except that the tailback should run to the sideline before cutting up into the area outside the fullback. We use this and tell our quarterback that it is a pass-run-pass pattern. The sprint out is taught as a run-pass and we find that in many cases the quarterback will run rather than pass. With the 141 call, the quarterback knows that we want the pass if at all possible, and as a last resort he can run.

Play Call: Right or Left 141 Option (Diagram 11-5 and 11-6)

Coaching Points: The diagrams might be a little bit misleading on this particular pass play. Once the quarterback clears the fullback, he will stand tall and throw the football. We are trying to catch the defense in a rotation or a retreat to cover pass. The tailback runs a flare pattern on this route and is also a possible

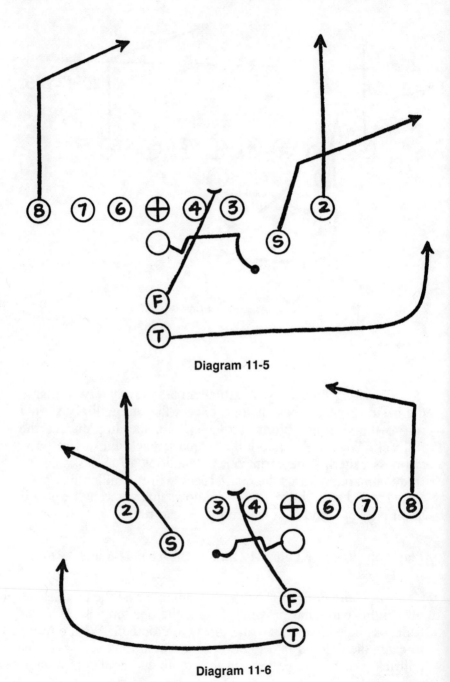

Diagram 11-5

Diagram 11-6

quick receiver. If the ball is thrown to the tailback in the short flat, the slotback and the 2 end peel back and block and we have a good running play with downfield blocking. As with any play-action pass, it is necessary to make the complementary running play go successfully before the pass pattern will work for your offense.

Play Call: Right or Left 233 (Diagrams 11-7 and 11-8)

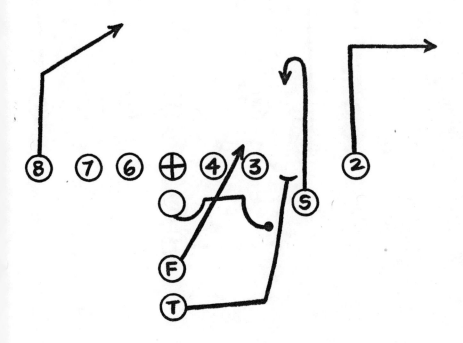

Diagram 11-7

Coaching Points: As with many of our pass patterns, we like to use the 33 action with the pass pattern. This type of action gives us a fake to the fullback and also the possibility of some protection from our tailback.

Diagram 11-8

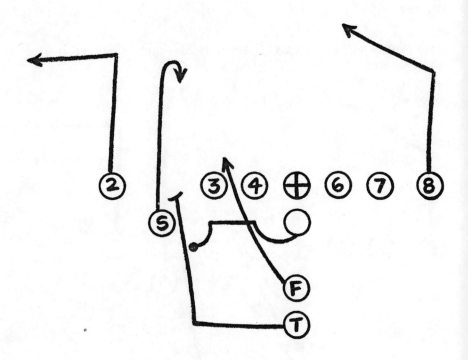

Play Call: Right or Left 232 (Diagrams 11-9 and 11-10)

Coaching Points: This is a very good action pass against those defenses that are keying very heavily on the tailback. The misdirection of the tailback causes enough indecision by the linebackers to open up the slotback on the hook. As you will see later, we do run a screen pass off this 32 action.

Diagram 11-9

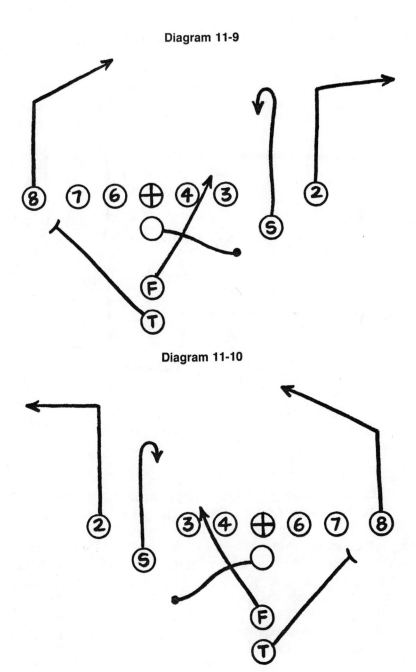

Diagram 11-10

Play Call: Right or Left 333: (Diagrams 11-11 and 11-12)

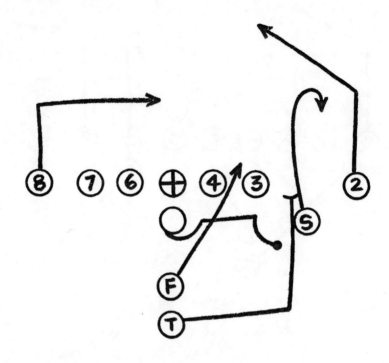

Diagram 11-11

Coaching Points: After our opponents see us play a few games, they know that we like to throw to the slot side more often than to the tight-end side. In fact, most of our pass patterns are designed to throw to the two-receiver side. The 300 pattern was designed to clear the area with the 2 end and, as the defense covers the slotback, to hit the 8 end coming through the middle. The 8 end goes approximately 8 yards in depth then comes toward the slot side looking for the pass anytime he is open in the middle of the defense. If he is not open, then he should continue on across looking for a possible downfield block. This 33 back-field action, which is used quite often, will be used for a draw

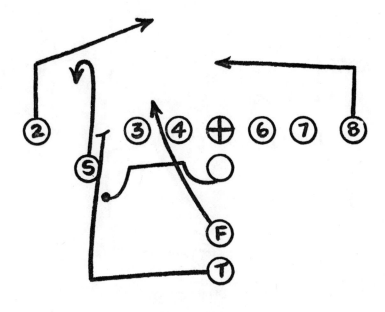

Diagram 11-12

play also. After the quarterback fish-hooks, he will hand the ball to the tailback as he comes up. The tailback must cut toward the line of scrimmage a little quicker than he normally would.

Play Call: Right or Left 433: (Diagrams 11-13 and 11-14)

Coaching Points: This is a very good pattern against the nine-man fronts with only two-deep secondary. We like to use the blue formation which splits both ends from 10 to 12 yards with this pattern. The 2 and 8 end go downfield 10 yards and run sideline patterns, taking the defensive halfbacks to the sidelines. The slotback then comes down the middle and is usually wide open. A good fake to the fullback will freeze the linebacker long enough to let the slotback get a two-step lead and into the open. This pattern has given us more touchdown passes than any other one that we use.

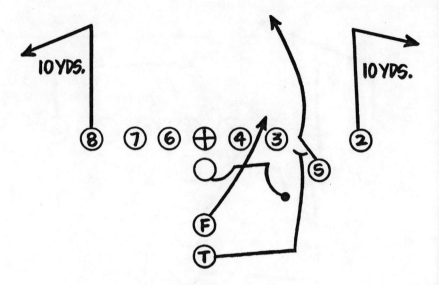

Diagram 11-13

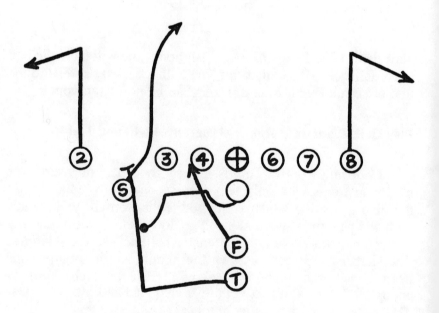

Diagram 11-14

Play Call: Right or Left 447: (Diagrams 11-15 and 11-16)

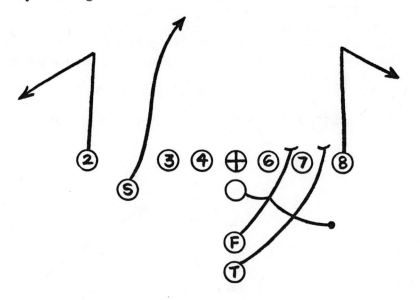

Diagram 11-15

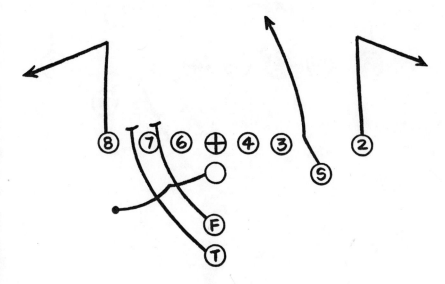

Diagram 11-16

Coaching Points: Our 447 pattern has also been a good pattern against the two-deep secondaries. The ends run the sideline patterns, pulling the halfbacks out, and the slotback again goes down the middle. By faking the 47, which we run quite often, we again freeze the linebackers long enough for the slotback to get open.

Play Call: Right or Left 842 (Diagrams 11-17 and 11-18)

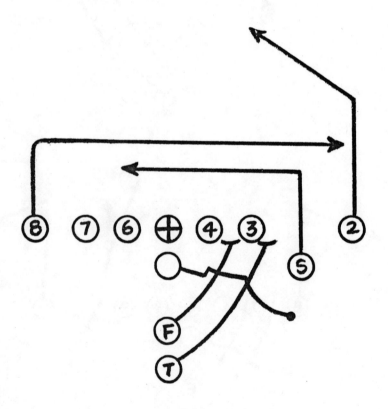

Diagram 11-17

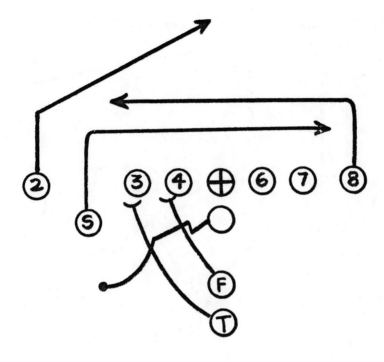

Diagram 11-18

Coaching Points: This is a very safe pass to throw. The primary receiver is the 8 end coming across under the coverage of the secondary and over the linebacker coverage. The fake of the 42 helps hold the linebackers at home and the crossing action of the slotback and the 8 end tends to free the 8 end. We also like to use the 33 action with this pattern, calling an 833. The 47 action with the 800 pattern makes a fine pattern also. The slotback is the primary receiver on the 847 but often the 2 end will be open deep, if the secondary reacts to the crossing pattern of the end and slotback.

Play Call: Right or Left 933 (Diagrams 11-19 and 11-20)

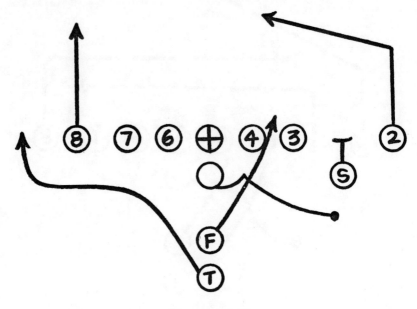

Diagram 11-19

Coaching Points: First of all, notice that on the 900 pattern, the slotback is not in the pattern. He stays at home and blocks. Also, notice that the tailback is in the pattern and goes opposite the quarterback for the throwback pass. The true backfield action is not a 33 as far as the tailback is concerned but for lack of a better call we use 33. The quarterback and the fullback still fake the 33 before the quarterback moves out to pass. We like the throwback action on occasion because it keeps the defense honest. This is a very good pass against a three-deep secondary that is rotating toward the quarterback's side. On rare occasions, we have let the fullback slide through to the flat area under the 2 end and thrown to him. This is a rather dangerous pattern to run, so you would probably not want to run the pattern too often. It is also a difficult pass for the quarterback because he must go out in one direction and throw back in the other direction. We always

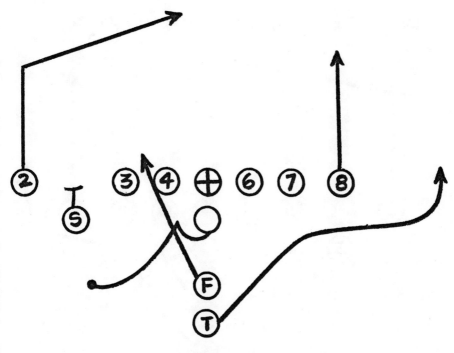

Diagram 11-20

want him to stop and step in the direction of the pass before he throws the football. Also, he is told that if any possible interceptor is in the area he should not throw the football. An interception of the throwback pass is almost a sure six points for the opponents.

The next pattern is one that we like to use quite often during the ball game. We have found that many defensive people key on our slotback to determine pass or run. If the slotback releases down the middle or into the flat, they read pass and if he stays at home and blocks, they read run. The 947, then, gives them a false key situation because the slotback will stay in and block even though we are running a pass pattern. We find that many secondary people key the slotback and if they come up on this particular pattern, then we can complete the deep pass to either the 2 end coming across the middle or to the 8 end going down the sideline.

Play Call: Right or Left 947 (Diagrams 11-21 and 11-22)

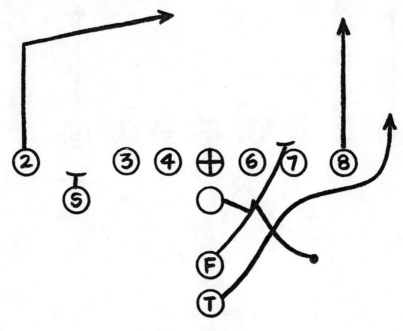

Diagram 11-21

Coaching Points: We try to get the backfield action to represent the 47 as long as is possible. The tailback should follow the fullback as in a 47 and at the last possible moment swing out into the flat area. The quarterback should make a good fake to the fullback then drop or fish-hook back and dump the ball to the tailback in the flat. This is a very short pass, probably about 5-7 yards from the quarterback to the tailback, and should be lobbed to the tailback over the defensive end and linebackers. The tailback should look over his inside shoulder to catch the ball so that he can see any possible interceptor.

On many occasions, we have found the secondary and linebackers coming up very fast to stop the 47 and have been able to throw the ball deep to either the 2 end or the 8 end. The

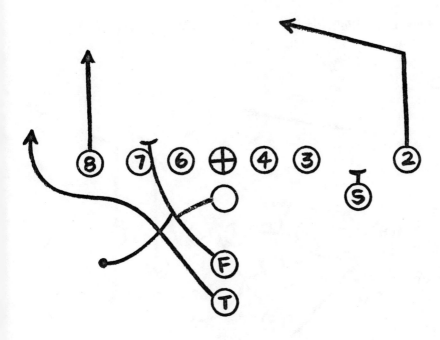

Diagram 11-22

quarterback should always make the 47 play go before he calls
the 947 pass. After several successful running plays in that direction, the pass play will also be quite successful.

SPECIAL PASS PLAYS

What we would like to cover in this little section are the
special plays that we have in our pass offense. By special plays
we mean our screen passes, our option passes thrown by the
tailback and the slotback, and the 43 draw play that we use.
Consider the screen passes first. We have two ways in
which we like to screen. One way is to throw a screen pass to the
tailback and the other is to throw the screen to our slotback. We
will diagram the screen pass to the tailback first and then draw
our screen pass to the slotback.

Play Call: Right or Left 232 Screen Pass (Diagrams 11-23 and 11-24)

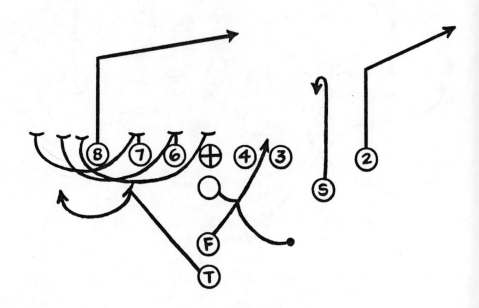

Diagram 11-23

Coaching Points: Although the screen pass can be run from any basic pattern, we use only the 200 pattern for simplicity. The 200 pattern sends out three receivers and thus occupies the secondary quite well. We use the 32 backfield action because the fullback and the tailback go in opposite directions. The fake to the fullback will freeze the linebackers long enough for the screen to set up. The tailback should block the defensive end for one count, as he would do on the 232, and then slide outside of the defensive end. He should look over his inside shoulder for the football. Once he has the ball he yells "Ball" so the linemen can release downfield to block for him.

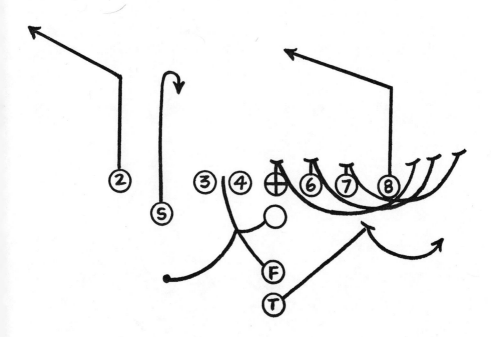

Diagram 11-24

The offensive linemen who are forming the screen, the 7 tackle, the 6 guard, and the 5 center, should block on the line of scrimmage for two counts before pulling toward the sideline to form the screen. They must not be allowed to pull downfield. We teach them to pull slightly away from the line of scrimmage to prevent the penalty for an ineligible receiver downfield. As they are pulling to the sideline, they should block any opponent who crosses their path. They must be taught not to let any defensive personnel leak through the screen and intercept the pass from the quarterback.

The quarterback, after making a good fake to the fullback, should come back slightly deeper than he normally would, then turn and throw the football over to the tailback behind the screen. The quarterback's pass should be a lob pass that is easy for the tailback to handle. The quarterback should follow his pass toward the tailback in case there is an interception. Timing is very important on the screen pass and should be worked on often.

The other screen pass that we use is to the slotback. We have been very successful with it and probably use it more than the tailback screen because so many people are keying heavily on the tailback.

Play Call: Right or Left 947 Screen Pass: (Diagrams 11-25 and 11-26)

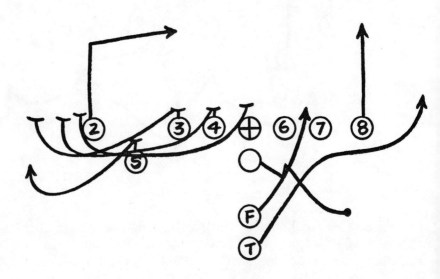

Diagram 11-25

Coaching Points: We use the 947 action for the slotback screen because the backfield action is going away from the slotback and the slotback blocks on the 900 pattern. The slotback should block for one count and then release into the flat area. He should be looking over his inside shoulder for the pass from the

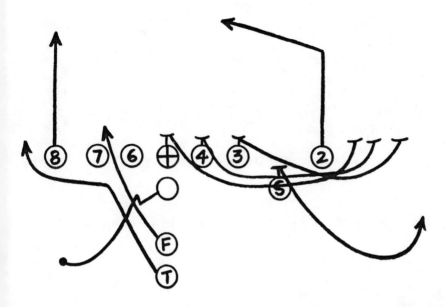

Diagram 11-26

quarterback. He must make sure that he is 3 to 4 yards behind the line of scrimmage so that the linemen in front of him will not be downfield. After catching the ball he yells "Ball" which will release the linemen in the screen downfield.

The screen is formed by the 3 tackle, the 4 guard, and the 5 center. They should block for two counts then pull slightly backward toward the sideline and in front of the slotback. They should block any opponent who comes into their area.

The backfield action is the same as in the 947 pass. The quarterback should fake to the fullback then hook back and lob the ball to the slotback. The tailback runs the same route that he does on the 947 pass, swinging out into the flat a little earlier for the secondary to see.

We have two plays in which backs other than the quarterback throw the ball. For lack of a fancy name, we simply call them 41 pass and 19 fly pass. On the 41 pass, we let the tailback throw the football and on the 19 fly pass we let the slotback throw the football. We use the 41 pass quite often and have been very successful with it because it looks as if we are running the sweep until, at the last moment, the tailback will stop and throw the football.

The 19 fly pass is not used as often as the 41 pass but it also has been very successful for us in the past few years. Both the tailback and the slotback must be instructed and constantly reminded not to throw the football if there is the slightest chance of a possible interception.

We will now diagram both of these passes from both a right and a left formation. The 41 pass is diagrammed first and then the 19 fly pass.

Play Call: Right or Left 41 Pass (Diagrams 11-27 and 11-28)

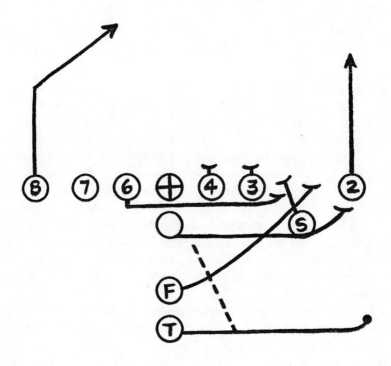

Diagram 11-27

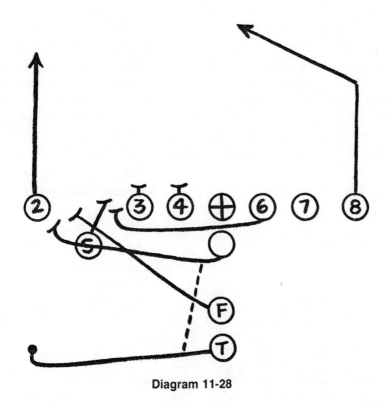

Diagram 11-28

Coaching Points: We block the 41 pass with the same rules that the 41 uses except when the linemen hear pass they do not go downfield. The slotback stays and blocks so we have only a two-receiver pattern. The ball usually is thrown to the 2 end on a streak pattern behind the defensive secondary. Once we have established the 41 in our running game, the secondary reacts very quickly to the 41 action and this allows the 2 end to get behind the defenders. It also works in reverse; if they have been staying back to protect against the pass it makes the 41 running play a better gainer. It is a very good play to keep the linebackers and secondary honest.

The 6 guard will pull as he does on the 41 but he will not turn upfield. If there is no one for him to pick up on the play side, he will turn to the back side and take any back-side rush. The 7 tackle must pull and seal for the 6 guard. The rest of the offensive linemen will block gap, over, fill area. Remember they cannot release downfield until the ball is thrown.

The backfield action is strictly the 41 action. The quarterback should reverse pivot, pitch, and lead-block for the tailback. The fullback should block the defensive end just as he does on the 41. The tailback should make the play look like the 41 until the last possible moment and then set up to throw. He also has the option of running with the football if none of the receivers is open. It is a very good play either way, pass or run.

Play Call: Right or Left 19 Fly Pass (Diagrams 11-29 and 11-30)

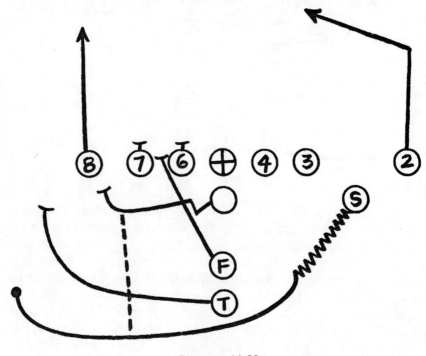

Diagram 11-29

Coaching Points: The 19 fly pass is used as a surprise element but is not used very often. It would not be used in every ball game but, as a special play, it has produced some fine results. Again, it must be set up with the 19 running play before

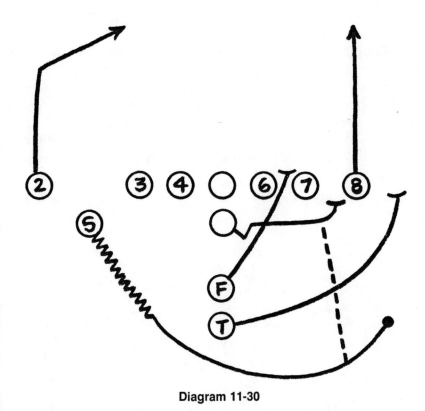

Diagram 11-30

it will be very effective. The word "fly" merely tells the slot-back to come in motion so that he can be in a good relationship with the quarterback and tailback, making it look like the running play. We have on a few occasions let the fullback slide out into the flat area if there are no linebackers trying to scrape through the line. He must make a good fake with the quarterback first. The tailback should block the defensive end because the quarterback is not optioning the end but rather pitching the ball after the fullback has cleared. The quarterback should help block after the pitch is made.

The linemen should block aggressively to make the play look like a run but must be reminded not to go downfield until the ball has been thrown. The 5 center should pull and take any back-side rush if he does not have any defensive people in his immediate area. The rest of the linemen merely block gap, over, fill area until the ball is thrown.

To make the play action passing attack complete, we add the draw play. In Chapter 9, Diagrams 9-7 and 9-8, we diagrammed our 41 draw which is actually a sprint-out draw play. We use almost the same action in our play-action draw which we call a 43 draw for lack of a better name. The quarterback and fullback use 33 action with the quarterback making a good fake to the fullback before he retreats and hands off to the tailback.

Play Call: Right or Left 43 Draw (Diagrams 11-31 and 11-32)

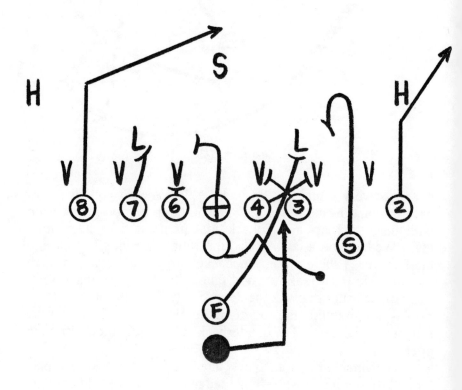

Diagram 11-31

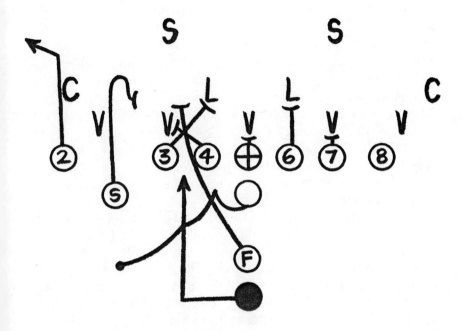

Diagram 11-32

Blocking Rules For 43 Draw

> 2 End—release downfield on a flag pattern, responsible for your half-back
>
> 3 Tackle—cross block with 4 guard, block man over 4
>
> 4 Guard—cross block with 3 tackle, block man outside 3
>
> 5 Center—over, weak-side linebacker
>
> 6 Guard—over, fill area
>
> 7 Tackle—over, linebacker, fill area
>
> 8 End—release downfield about 10 yards the cut and block the safety
>
> Fullback—block on linebacker after faking a 33
>
> Slotback—release down the middle and hook back blocking any offside pursuit
>
> Tailback—take three steps toward the sideline, square to line of scrimmage, take handoff, and run to daylight
>
> Quarterback—reverse pivot and fake a 33 with fullback, square to sideline, hand to tailback, continue on back as if to pass

Coaching Points: The line blocking on the 43 draw is exactly the same as on the 41 draw to make things simple for the linemen. Once they hear the word "Draw" they know what the blocking assignment will be no matter what play number has been called.

After faking the 33, the fullback should block the first other-colored jersey that he sees. It is important for him to fake the 33 well into the line of scrimmage before looking for someone to block. This will freeze the linebacker and make the block easier for the fullback or the 3 tackle, depending upon the defense. If no defensive man shows up for the fullback to block, he should lead the tailback downfield.

The cross block between the 3 tackle and the 4 guard is very important. The 3 tackle should always go first, in front of the 4 guard. The 4 guard should then pull to the outside and block the man over or outside of the 3 tackle. On some defenses, such as the 4-4 stack, he may be responsible for a linebacker in his area.

In concluding this chapter, remember that what we have diagrammed for you is only a small part of what can be done as far as play action passes are concerned. By combining the six basic pass routes (100, 200, 300, 400, 800, 900) with the great number of backfield actions, the play-action passing attack is almost unlimited. What we have tried to do is to show you the passes that we use most often. We feel that our method of calling and executing play-action passes is a very simple but yet sound method. The passing game is merely a complement to our Slot I running game. The passing attack includes the screens, draws, and special passes that can be learned very quickly and only have to be practiced occasionally to be remembered. We spend approximately 20 to 30 minutes each practice session on our passing game.

12

The Complete Kicking Game
for the Slot I Offense

Probably the most neglected phase of football is the kicking game. Coaches spend numerous hours studying and diagramming offenses and defenses but often overlook the kicking game which, we feel, is one of the most important parts of football. Without a sound kicking game, we feel we cannot be a sound football team. In our daily practice schedule, we have a 15-minute period in which we work entirely on some aspect of our kicking game. Our kicking period used to be at the end of practice, immediately before our conditioning period, but we found that the players tended to loaf because of the upcoming sprints. We moved it and now have our kicking period early in our daily practice schedule, right after our agility period and before our individual work. The players are fresh and will work very hard on the kicking game at this time. We also like it early in the practice schedule because it involves quite a lot of running and, therefore, it serves as a good warm-up along with another conditioning period.

What we will do in this chapter is to cover our complete kicking game including punts, punt returns, kickoffs, kickoff returns, onside kick, quick kick, and field goal or P.A.T.'s. We consider punt returns and kickoff returns as great offensive weapons because we are attempting to advance the football. Likewise, the punts, kickoffs, quick kicks, and field goals are also offensive weapons. On what other offensive play are you assured of gaining at least 35 yards or more? Just think about that again, for a minute—on how many offensive running or passing plays are you assured of at least 35 yards? The kicking game is surely a great offensive weapon if it is used correctly and executed properly.

The principal part of the kicking game is your punt formation. There are several aspects to the punting game and, in the next few pages, we will cover it from basic alignment through the punt coverage.

Punt Formation (Diagram 12-1)

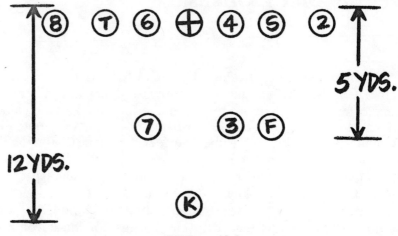

Diagram 12-1

Look closely at Diagram 12-1. Notice that on the line of scrimmage, the slotback has taken the space normally occupied by the 3 tackle and that the tailback has taken the space normally occupied by the 7 tackle. The tackles along with the fullback make up the second wall, five yards deep. We do this for two reasons. First, it gives us more speed on the coverage by having the slotback and the tailback going downfield from the line of scrimmage and second, it gives us greater protection for the kicker by having the large tackles immediately in front of him. After the ball has been hiked, the two tackles will slide together to protect the kicker further. One important coaching point—if your kicker is left-footed, have the fullback line up next to the 7 tackle instead of next to the 3 tackle. This gives added protection on the side of the kicking foot.

The basic splits along the line of scrimmage are 1 yard, 1 yard, 1 yard. The feet of the 4 guard should be 1 yard from the feet of the center, the slotback's feet 1 yard from the 4 guard's feet, etc.

The second wall, the two tackles and the fullback, should be 5 yards behind the line of scrimmage and foot-to-foot. They should have absolutely no splits between them once the ball has been hiked. It is the responsibility of the tackles to make sure the ball gets by them to the kicker. It is the tackles' fault if the center hits either of them with the hike.

The kicker should be 12 yards in depth and immediately behind the center. It is his responsibility to make sure there is enough room between the two tackles for the ball to be hiked.

The punting unit has two responsibilities. The first is to protect the kicker and the second is to cover the punt downfield. Let's look at these two things individually.

PUNT PROTECTION

We number the defensive personnel, linemen and linebackers, from the outside in. We then give the following rules to our linemen:

> 2 End—number 1 on your side
>
> Slotback—number 2 on your side
>
> 4 Guard—number 3 on your side
>
> Center—hike the ball and do not worry about blocking anyone
>
> 6 Guard—number 3 on your side
>
> Tailback—number 2 on your side
>
> 8 End—number 1 on your side

As you can see if the defense rushes with more than 6 people we want this rush, the extra people, to come through the middle. By funneling them through the middle, they must then go through our secondary wedge to block the football. We think that most punts are blocked by some speedster coming around the outside, so we protect against this.

The three people in the secondary wedge, the two tackles and the fullback, are responsible for anyone coming through the middle. They should not step to the outside unless this is the only place a rush is coming from. For example, the fullback should stay next to the tackle and not go outside after a rusher unless the fullback sees that this is the only person rushing the punter. If a fullback turns out and someone gets between him and the tackle, then the punt will be blocked. Believe me, if a punt is blocked because the fullback turns out he will not be around on the next punting situation.

The secondary wedge is also instructed not to give ground. If they back up the least bit, the kicker is liable to kick the ball into one of them and we are then blocking our own punt.

The kicker, of course, must first of all field the snap no matter where it happens to be. He then should help the protection by stepping directly forward as he kicks and not to the side. As coaches, we must make sure that the kicker is going forward and not stepping to the side before he kicks the football. If he steps sideways, he could possibly be going away from his protection. If he is going away from the protection, then there is a greater chance of the kick being blocked.

Punt Coverage: (Diagram 12-2)

On our punt coverage, each player on the line of scrimmage must block for two counts before releasing downfield on the punt coverage. The secondary wedge must block until the ball is kicked to protect the kicker in case of a bad snap from center.

Our basic punt coverage rules are simple and easily understood. We have no crossing, etc. in our coverage. Each individual is responsible for a certain area and must be drilled so that he covers the proper area without even thinking about it.

The ends, 2 and 8, are our containment men on the punt. They are responsible for keeping everything inside of themselves and not letting the opponents get their return started up the sideline.

The slotback and the tailback are our headhunters in the punt formation. They are free to move downfield to try to make

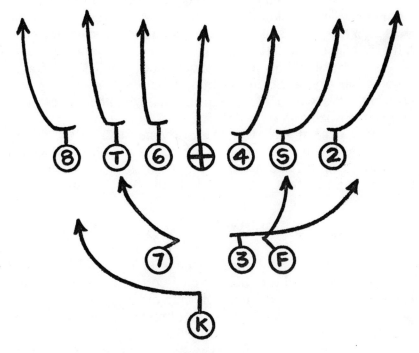

Diagram 12-2

the tackle before the return is set up. They are our fastest people so they normally get downfield the farthest, the fastest. We want them to be approximately 7 to 10 yards from the sidelines as they move down the field and at the last moment they should get under control and move in for the tackle.

The guards and the center are usually slower than the ends and the backs so they will cover down the middle of the field after releasing from the line of scrimmage. The center, because he has no blocking responsibility, can often get down the middle almost as quick as the slotback and the tailback and give us quick support in the middle of the field.

From the secondary wedge, the 7 tackle and the fullback cover downfield behind the slotback and the tailback. They will not leave until the ball is kicked, so they act like the trailers on a fast break in basketball. They should always be under control and then move into the football.

The 3 tackle and the punter serve as safety men for the punt formation. The 3 tackle should cover down the right side of the field after the ball is kicked and the punter should cover down the left side of the field once the ball is kicked. They are the safety men so they should always be under control and should not be involved in any tackles if the front people are doing their jobs correctly. We would like to go all season without these two people ever being in on a tackle.

As a general rule, we have everyone block at the line of scrimmage for two counts, then sprint downfield for 30 yards, get under control, and move to the football. A most important point is to have them sprint, not loaf, the first 30 yards.

QUICK KICK

One of the best surprise weapons in our whole offensive attack is our quick kick. If employed correctly, the quick kick can gain a great deal of yardage for the offensive unit. You will probably say to yourself, this is true, but you are also giving up the football to the opponent. In response to such a statement, we would reply that we strongly believe in field-position football. We are confident that our defense will get the football back for us and, therefore, we hope to improve our field position on the exchange of kicks. We are not afraid to use the quick kick on any part of the field and will often quick kick on second down when we are deep in our own territory. We have even quick kicked on first down, depending upon field position, score, and quarter in the game.

On the quick kick, the tailback does the kicking so we use our basic I formation. If the tailback is right-footed, you should use a right formation, and if he is left-footed you should use a left formation. We do this to get the extra blocking by the slotback on the side the kicker uses.

What we will do now is to diagram the basic quick kick, then give the blocking rules for it, and finally describe the coverage for it. We will assume that the tailback is a right-footed kicker and diagram the quick kick from a right formation.

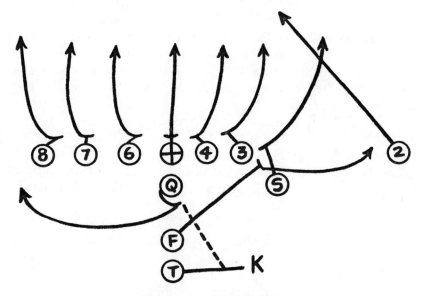

Diagram 12-3: Quick Kick

Blocking Rules for the Quick Kick

2 End—release directly to the football

3 Tackle—protect gap, over, then release downfield

4 Guard—protect gap, over, then release downfield

5 Center—fill area, then release downfield

6 Guard—gap, over, release downfield

7 Tackle—gap, over, release downfield

8 End—gap, over, release downfield

Slotback—protect gap, over, fill area, then release downfield

Fullback—protect on outside hip of slotback

Tailback—take two or three steps as on a 41 then stop and kick

Quarterback—reverse pivot and pitch the ball as on a 41 then cover opposite direction

Coaching Points: There are several very important items if the quick kick is to be executed properly. Probably, the most important is that the backfield action look like the 41 until the last possible moment. We do not want the defensive secondary to be dropping back and returning the football. The quarterback should reverse pivot and pitch the ball as he would on a 41 and he should not move opposite until the tailback is about set to kick. The quarterback will then become the safety on the weak side and he should trail the offensive linemen by about 10 yards as they release down the field.

The fullback must seal at the outside hip of the slotback and not let anyone penetrate through this area. He must not allow a defender to drive him backward because he will be in the way of the tailback's kick. Once the ball is kicked, the fullback becomes the safety on the strong side and he should trail the linemen by approximately 10 yards as they cover downfield.

The tailback starts toward the sideline as on a 41 and after receiving the pitch should pull up and kick the ball. The technique used by the tailback to kick the ball is an important one. We want the ball to roll after it hits the ground to gain added yardage. We will try to describe the kicking technique that we have our tailback use. As he kicks the ball, the tailback should be facing the sideline. The ball should be held by the points with the laces up and parallel to the sideline. The tailback should kick the ball on its back half. Kicked in this manner, the ball will have an end-over-end rotation and will bounce and roll for several yards after it hits the ground. The ball should be kicked as high as possible and still have the correct rotation for the forward roll. The rolling can often carry farther than the kick itself.

With a little practice, the tailback should consistently get 40 yards with his quick kick and can possibly get even farther on an average. We have had one tailback average 54 yards on his quick kicks, with his farthest being 80 yards. It can be a great way of moving the football down the field.

As far as the linemen are concerned, they should protect the inside gap first, block man over if no one is in the gap, or fill the area until the ball is kicked. They then release downfield approximately 7 to 10 yards apart and move to the football. The 2 end is the headhunter and he should release from the line of scrimmage immediately and go for the football. He should down the football if it starts rolling back upfield. We like to use a RED formation for our quick kick so that the 2 end is split and cannot be jammed on the line of scrimmage. He must never let the ball be returned by the defensive secondary.

The 8 end and the slotback will serve as containment men if the ball should happen to be returned. They will funnel the ball back into the middle of the field to where there is help.

All personnel should block on the line of scrimmage, except the 2 end, for two counts or until the ball is kicked. The tailback should yell ''Ball'' once it has been kicked and the linemen should yell ''right, left, or middle'' to help the 2 end locate the ball as he sprints down the field.

THE KICKOFF

Another important part of the kicking game is the kickoff. Either at the start of the game or at the beginning of the second half, you are going to have to kickoff to your opponents. Also, after each scoring play you will have to kickoff to them. The kickoff is very important because you do not want your opponent to have good field position because of poor kickoffs and poor kickoff coverage.

What we will do now is to give you our kickoff alignment and coverage. We do something on the kickoff that is unique to most kickoffs. We have seen very few teams that do not kickoff from the middle of the field so we want to be slightly different and make our opponents prepare a little extra before they play us. We place and kick the ball from the right hash mark. As far as advantages to this, we must admit, in all honesty, that there are only a few. We mentioned that the opponent must prepare to receive the kick from the right hash mark so they must spend some extra time practicing their returns from this position. This, in turn, means that they must slight some other phase of their game to practice a return from the right hash mark. Also, we feel that they can return only to our left or to the wide side of the field. If they return to our right, they will be contained by the short sideline area.

Probably, the most important reason for kicking from the

right hash mark is that it has improved our onside kicking game.
We like to onside kick into the right sideline where most teams
leave a slight opening. We have found that many teams like to
line up as if the ball will be kicked into the middle with their front
five linemen, thus leaving the sideline open for the onside kick.

Whether the kicking from the right hash mark is really that
advantageous is questionable, but we like it and will continue to
do it that way.

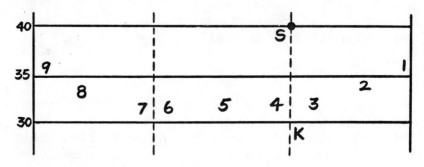

Diagram 12-4

Kickoff Alignment

Most coaches have special kickoff teams, so we just number
our personnel from 1 through 9, plus the kicker and a safety. We
have all our people, number 1 through number 9, face in toward
the football. They use a two-point stance with hands on the
knees. As they see the person immediately inside of them pass,
they will move on downfield. What is a "V" type of alignment
becomes a straight line as they near the football.

We call numbers 2, 8, and the kicker headhunters. They are
to get downfield to the football as soon as possible. These are the
reckless individuals. They should not worry about missing tackles, etc., but merely get to the football as soon as possible.
Notice that we have a headhunter in each area or one-third of the
field. Number 2 is in the right third, the kicker in the middle
third, and number 8 is in the left third. It is surprising how many
times in a season these three individuals spoil the return before it
gets started.

Our other people, numbers 1, 3, 4, 6, 7, 9, we call campers.

They are to sprint to the 30-yard line as fast as possible, then balance up and get under control. Once they are under control, they should move on to the football being careful not to let the ball carrier pass them. They should not stop at the 30, but merely slow up and get ready to hit people. Numbers 1 and 9 are the containment people and must never allow people to get outside of them. They should turn everything back into the middle where they have additional help.

Our Number 5 acts as a safety. He should move to our opponent's 40-yard line and in the middle of the field so that he can cover either way. He should look for the ball carrier and cut him off should he get past our campers.

Our safety should go to the 50-yard line and into the middle of the field. He has the same responsibilities as Number 5 and is the last possible tackler should a return break through our campers. The safety and Number 5 should be excellent open-field tacklers, have good speed, etc. We hope that they never have to make a tackle, but if the occasion arises, they can save the 6 points if they are capable open-field tacklers.

Notice in the kickoff coverage (Diagram 12-5), the spacing between the players. The spacing is very important if you are to cover the entire field. There are two campers assigned to each one-third of the field. Their spacing should constantly be checked to make sure they are covering in the correct third.

We are so confident of our kickoff coverage and our defense that we often kickoff to start the game, rather than receive, if we have our choice. This then serves two purposes. One, we will get the football back in good field position. If we receive, we have to start around our own 20- to 30-yard line. And second, we get rid of the opening jitters by getting the first hits. We do not have to handle the ball and give up the football by way of a fumble because of the jitters. We feel that we have a very fine and capable offense but why go against the percentages.

ONSIDE KICK

We have had great success with our onside kick over the past few years. We use the same alignment that we use on a

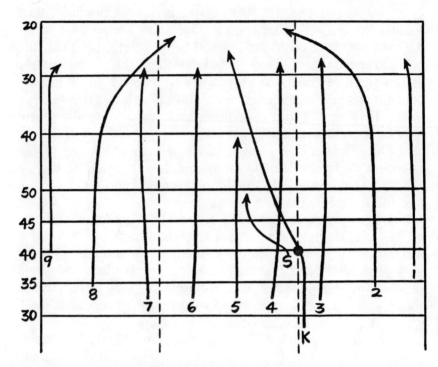

Diagram 12-5: Kickoff Coverage

kickoff (Diagram 12-4). We tell our personnel the following things.

No. 1—recover the football, do not let it roll out of bounds, be reckless and gamble

No. 2—block first man in from sideline, trying to keep him from getting the football

No. 3—block second man in from the sideline, trying to keep him from getting the football

K—block third man in from the sideline, trying to keep him from getting the football

S—you are the kicker, try to place the ball about half way between the sideline and the hash mark, about 11 yards deep. Follow your kick and help Number 1 in any manner possible.

No.'s 5 and 8—you are safety men. Turn and cover to the right
   sideline against a possible return up the sideline

No.'s 4, 6, 7, 9—you are campers and should cover downfield
   against a return in your direction. Do not cover deeper than
   the ball

Applying the rules that we have just given, we would have
an onside kick as in Diagram 12-6.

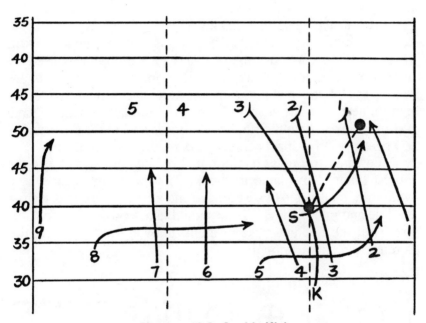

Diagram 12-6: Onside Kick

A very important part of any successful onside kick is that it
looks like a regular kickoff until the last possible moment. The
kicker and the other nine people should be approaching the 40
before the safety kicks the ball. The safety must be careful and
not let them be offside before he kicks the football. When he

kicks the football, we like to have the safety hit its top half and have it roll the 10 yards rather than kick it in the air. If it is rolling, it is harder to field and it takes longer to reach the 10 or 11 yards necessary. This type of kick also allows the Number 1 more time to get downfield and cover the football.

Another aspect of the onside kick is that it can be used at any time in a ball game. It should not be used only late in the fourth quarter when you are behind and everyone in the ball park knows that it is coming. It can be successful as a surprise element at any point in the ball game.

The last part of the kicking game that we would like to cover, before we get into our returns, is the field goal or extra point formation. We use the standard formation that is used by almost every football coach in the nation. The extra points are vital parts of the kicking game because they can provide the margin necessary for victory. If you are fortunate enough to have a strong kicker, then the field goal affords a team the opportunity to score if a drive has been stopped short of the goal line.

For the extra point or field goal protection, we will use the largest linemen available to block. The big linemen give us a wide front on the line of scrimmage and are very hard to drive off the line and into the kick. They should take a position of foot-to-foot with the linemen next to them, allowing no gaps that the defense can shoot through.

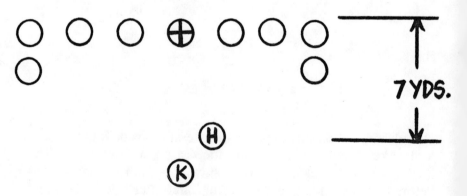

Diagram 12-7: Field Goal and Extra Point

The rules for the linemen on extra points, and field goals are very simple. On the snap of the ball, come up and protect your inside gap. They must never turn to the inside, however, and create a hole for the defense. Stay square and as big as possible.

If the ball is poorly snapped, we have the holder and the kicker yell "Help" and our ends and backs release for a possible pass from one of them. A broken play can often turn into a 2-point conversion. The release routes are shown in Diagram 12-8.

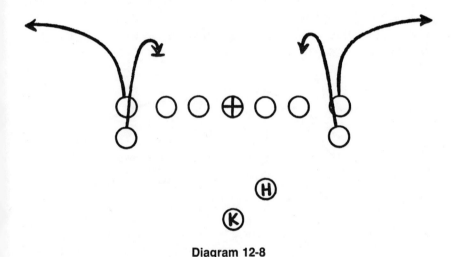

Diagram 12-8

We would like now to spend the rest of this chapter covering our kick-return game. A well organized and executed return, whether a punt return or a kickoff return, can give the offense the good field position from which to start its drive or, in some cases, may present a score on its own.

PUNT RETURN

Well executed punt returns have broken up many football games. To be effective on a punt return, your return team must take pride in blocking for the returner and you must have a good punt returner. To be a good punt returner, we feel, a player should have good speed, agility, toughness, and a certain amount of downright recklessness. He must be confident to catch the ball in a crowd and also possess a certain amount of intelligence so that he knows when to catch the ball, when to fair catch the ball, and when not to catch the ball.

Defensively, we play a basic Notre Dame Split-Six and a 4-4- Stack. When it is a kicking down, we jump into our split-six defense and run our punt return out of the 6-2-3 alignment. So that we don't look the same every time, we will return either right or left. What we will do now is to diagram the right return, giving the rules and assignments, then the left return, giving its rules and assignments.

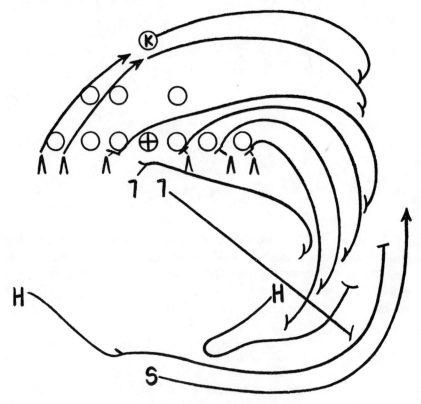

Diagram 12-9: Punt Return Right

Alignment

Front Six Defensive Personnel—normal split-six alignment

Linebackers—normal split-six defensive alignment

Halfbacks—20 to 25 yards deep

Safety—35 to 40 yards deep, depending upon the ability of the kicker; you may have to be deeper

Responsibility

Right End—Drive your inside shoulder into the offensive end to slow him down, then peel back to the right. You will lead the wall to within five yards of the football and about ten yards from the right sideline. Once the ball is caught, you should turn inside and block toward the left sideline, forming approximately a 45-degree angle with it.

Right Tackle—Drive your shoulder into the offensive tackle to slow him down, then peel back to the right and follow your offensive end back to the football. You should be approximately five yards from the end but do not let anyone run between you and the end.

Right Guard—Drive your shoulder into the offensive guard to slow him down, then peel back to the right and follow your defensive tackle back to the football. You should be approximately five yards from the tackle.

Left Guard—Drive your inside shoulder into the offensive guard to slow him down, then peel back to the right and follow the other guard back to the football. You should be approximately five yards from the guard.

Left Tackle—You are responsible for putting pressure on the kicker. You should fire through and block the kick if at all possible. Once the ball has been kicked, you should go to the right and get into the wall next to the guard. Primary responsibility is pressure on the kicker.

Left End—You are responsible for putting pressure on the kicker. You should fire through and block the kick if at all possible. Once the ball has been kicked, you should go to the right and get into the wall next to the tackle. Primary responsibility is pressure on the kicker.

Right Linebacker—Once the ball is snapped, turn and immediately go downfield to the football. You are responsible for the first offen-

sive man downfield, usually the offensive end, and should block
him toward the sideline. You are to kick the widest man out.

Left Linebacker—On the snap of the football, you should drive a shoulder into the offensive center to slow him up. You then should peel
back to the right and block in the wall formed by the defensive
linemen. Check to make sure it is not a fake punt before leaving.

Halfbacks—Fair catch any punt in front of you. Watch for a fake punt
and a run or pass. Always check the route of the offensive ends as
they come down the field for a possible pass play. Once the ball
has been kicked over your head, turn and go to protect the safety.
Tell the safety to fair catch or not. Once the ball is caught, lead the
ball carrier up and through the wall. Block only those who are
challenging your position in front of the ball carrier. If you are the
halfback away from the wall, you will really have to sprint to get
ahead of the ball carrier.

Safety—Catch the football. Listen for help from the halfbacks as to fair
catch or not. Do not let the ball bounce unless it will go into the
end zone. If you are on the 10-yard line, let any ball over your
head go into the end zone unless you are positive that you can
return it past the 20-yard line.

Coaching Points: Always make sure the defensive linemen
and linebackers are driving the shoulder into the offensive man
before they peel back to block if their assignment calls for that
technique. We find that they often merely turn and run away,
which definitely invites the fake punt situation. They will not be
much help with their backs to the punter if he has not punted and
decides to run. Also, once they have peeled back they should
block across the field at an angle and not run ahead of the ball
carrier. If they block toward the line of scrimmage at an angle,
the pursuit of the kicking team will make their blocks simple.

As can be seen by looking at Diagram 12-10, our punt
return, left, is a mirror of the punt return, right. The alignments
for the left return are exactly the same as those for the right return
described earlier in the chapter. Also, the responsibilities for a
left return are just the reverse of the right return. For example, on
a left return the right defensive end and tackle would have the
same responsibilities that the left defensive end and tackle had on
the right return. On the left return, the rush responsibilities come

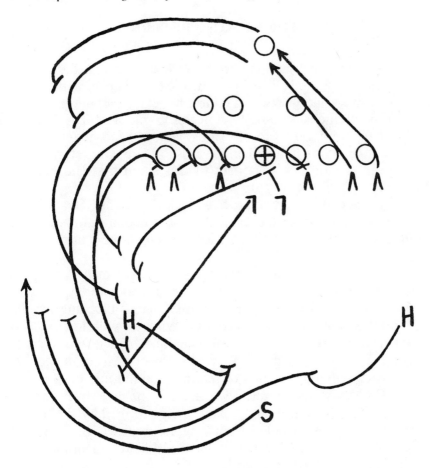

Diagram 12-10: Punt Return Left

from the right end and the right tackle. The wall is formed by the left end, tackle, guard, and the right guard. The left side linebacker will go directly downfield and kick the widest and deepest offensive player outside while the right side linebacker will drive a shoulder into the center and then get into the blocking wall.

The halfbacks and the safety have the same responsibilities as in a right return except that they will now run to the left after they have caught the football.

THE KICKOFF RETURN

Another important play for the offensive team is the kickoff return. Because we believe strongly in the field position theory of football, we want our kickoff returns to get the ball out to at least the 30-yard line and, hopefully, nearer to midfield. The chances of moving the football for 50 yards without a mistake are much greater than trying to go 70 or 80 yards to score. Our returns were designed to gain that important field position first and then, if possible, go all the way for a score.

We actually use two types of kickoff returns. The sideline return and a return up the middle. We use both a right and a left sideline return, so, actually, we are teaching three returns; right, left, and middle.

Let us consider the middle return first. For many years, we used wedge blocking for our middle return and were quite successful with it. The last year, we used a cross-blocking middle return that was also quite successful. What we will do now is to give you the two middle return techniques and let you decide which return you like the best. We do, however, recommend that you teach only one method of returning up the middle.

On the wedge return, we actually have a front wedge formed by the linemen and a back wedge formed by the backs. The center is responsible for forming the front wedge. Once the ball is kicked, the center and all linemen should turn and sprint to a position about 10 yards in front of the ball. The center is the apex of the wedge and the other linemen should form about him and as close to him as possible. After the wedge is properly formed, the linemen should turn and start upfield. In all probability, the center will block the kicker, the guards will block Number 1, the tackles will block Number 2, and the ends will block Number 3.

The back wedge is formed by the backs and should be within five yards of the football. The fullback is responsible for forming the apex and the slotback and the quarterback will align next to him. They will then follow the front wedge and help split the middle for the tailback to go through.

The important coaching point on a middle-wedge return is not to let any member of the kicking team split or go between any members of the wedge. This is a very simple return to teach and we have been quite successful in gaining the field position that we feel is necessary with a return.

The other return that we use in the middle of the field involves cross blocking by our guards and tackles. This type of return requires more speed in the front-five people than does the wedge return. The guards and tackles retreat and cross over to the other side to block.

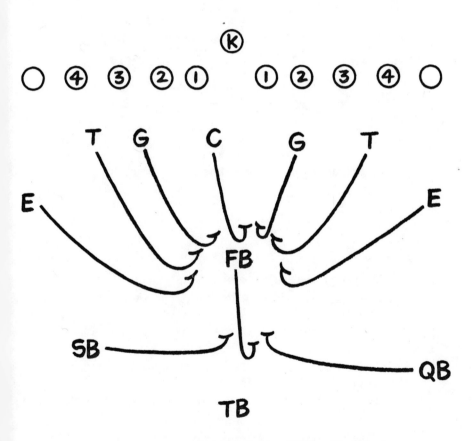

Diagram 12-11: The Middle Return (Wedge Blocking)

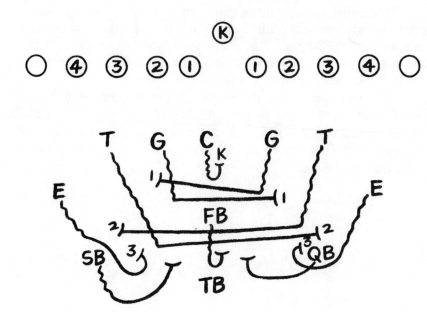

Diagram 12-12: Middle Return (Cross-Blocking)

Assignments for Cross-Blocking Middle Return:

Center—give ground and block the kicker.

Guards—give ground and block first man on opposite side of kicker from you

Tackles—give ground and block second man on opposite side of kicker from you

Ends—give ground toward the football and block the 3 man from the kicker, on your side, out

Fullback—give ground toward the tailback, then lead-block up the middle

Slotback and quarterback—give ground toward the tailback, then form a middle wedge with the fullback, and lead the tailback up the middle of the field

Tailback—catch the football and follow the other three backs up the middle of the field.

An important coaching point—once the ball carrier is by the wall of defenders, the wedge should break and peel back to block, letting the tailback go. On several occasions, our wedge would continue on down the field ahead of the tailback and he would be caught from behind because he could not get past our own blockers.

We like the middle return involving the cross-blocking technique best, but we do not always have the speed to use this technique. If your tackles are slightly slower than the guards, put the tackles on the inside and the guards on the outside. The quicker guards will then have the farthest to go for their blocks.

SIDELINE KICKOFF RETURNS

We employ two sideline returns, one right and one left. The two returns are very easily taught and can be very successful if they are executed properly.

Assignments for Sideline Return Right

Right Tackle—peel back to the right to within about 10 yards of the football and next to the end of your side. Block toward the left sideline

Right Guard—follow the right tackle and block back toward the left sideline

Center—follow the right guard and block back toward the left sideline

Left Guard—follow the center and block back toward the left sideline

Left Tackle—follow the left guard and block back toward the left sideline

Right End—turn and drop to within approximately seven yards of the football. You are the beginning of the wall and should be about ten yards in from the sideline. Turn in and block toward the left sideline.

Left End—your responsibility is the kicker—go and block him

Fullback—drop back to the football and then lead-block for the tailback up the outside of the wall

Quarterback—your job is to block the man responsible for containment out. Your block is the most important one and a good block will allow the tailback to turn the corner

Slotback—sprint across the field and lead-block for the tailback.

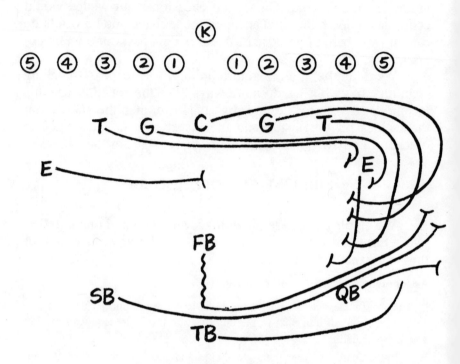

Diagram 12-13: Sideline Return Right

Coaching Points: If the kick is short and to the fullback, we allow him to do one of two things. First, he can pitch the ball back to the tailback and we will run the normal return or second, he can keep the ball and gain as much yardage as he possibly can by himself.

If the ball is kicked to the quarterback or to the person in the quarterback's place, we want him to pitch the ball back to the tailback and then take care of his normal responsibility. This block by the quarterback is vital for a good kickoff return.

If the ball goes to the slotback, then we merely lead with the tailback and let the slotback carry the football. It would be nice if every team kicked to the slotback because the tailback would already be ahead of the ball carrier, whereas the slotback must sprint to get in front of the tailback to be a lead blocker.

Assignments: The assignments for the left return simply mirror those of a right return. The front-five linemen will peel back to the left and block in toward the right sideline. The left end will become the lead blocker on the wall and the right end will be responsible for the kicker. The slotback will now block the containment man out and the quarterback will become a blocker, along with the fullback, ahead of the tailback.

Remember the kicking game can give your team that little bit extra that makes the difference between a good team and a championship team. Spend some time on the kicking game and you will readily see the results on the football field.

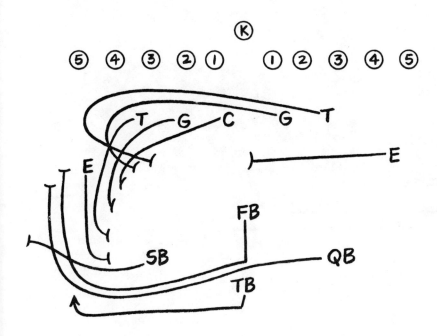

Diagram 12-14: Sideline Return Left

Index